COLLABORATIVE WRITING
PLAYBOOK

COLLABORATIVE WRITING PLAYBOOKS

Writing to Learn in Teams: A Collaborative Writing Playbook for Students Across the Curriculum

A book full of tools students will use for the rest of their lives whether they're writing to learn or learning to write in their disciplines. Includes student- and instructor-tested practices that expand capacities for productive collaborative writing in any genre.

Collaborative Writing at Work: A Playbook for Teams

A timely resource for any organization that wants to realize the full potential of a collaborative, connected, interdependent workplace. Combines the best of design thinking and agile principles to sustain productive, highly motivated teams.

COLLABORATIVE WRITING PLAYBOOK

AN INSTRUCTOR'S GUIDE TO DESIGNING
WRITING PROJECTS FOR STUDENT TEAMS

Joe Moses and Jason Tham

Parlor Press
Anderson, South Carolina
www.parlorpress.com

Parlor Press LLC, Anderson, South Carolina, USA

© 2021 by Parlor Press
All rights reserved.
Printed in the United States of America on acid-free paper.
S A N: 2 5 4 - 8 8 7 9

Library of Congress Cataloging-in-Publication Data on File

978-1-64317-239-2 (paperback)
978-1-64317-240-8 (pdf)
978-1-64317-241-5 (epub)

First Edition

1 2 3 4 5

Cover image: Used by permission.
Interior design by Jason Tham

Parlor Press, LLC is an independent publisher of scholarly and trade titles in print and multimedia formats. This book is available in paper and eBook formats from Parlor Press on the World Wide Web at http://www.parlorpress.com or through online and brick-and-mortar bookstores. For submission information or to find out about Parlor Press publications, write to Parlor Press, 3015 Brackenberry Drive, Anderson, South Carolina, 29621, or email editor@parlorpress.com.

CONTENTS

xiii   Preface
x   Acknowledgments
vi   Chapter overview
viii   List of tables
ix   List of figures

1   Introduction: Why collaborative writing matters
25   Chapter 1: What does a good collaborative writing project look like?
41   Chapter 2: How can collaborative writing support your course learning objectives?
63   Chapter 3: Collaborative writing roles and tasks for interdependent teamwork
89   Chapter 4: An interdependent learning environment for collaborative writing
107   Chapter 5: A writing process for interdependent collaboration
129   Chapter 6: Create a vision for collaborative writing

148   Final words
149   References
151   Keywords

CHAPTER OVERVIEW

CHAPTER | **GUIDING QUESTIONS**

1 What does a good collaborative writing project look like?
- What is collaborative writing?
- How can collaborative writing support my course learning objectives?
- What are structured activities?
- How can teams make meetings productive?

2 How can collaborative writing support your course learning objectives?
- Where does collaborative writing intersect with course learning objectives?
- What are my course objectives for critical thinking?
- What are my course objectives for research?
- What are my course objectives for genre/structure?
- What are my course objectives for synthesis?
- What are my course objectives for review/editing?

3 Collaborative writing roles and tasks for interdependent teamwork.
- How do I define teammate roles?
- How do I devise teammate tasks?
- How do I identify individual contributions to collaboratively written content?
- How do I assign teammate roles?

CHAPTER OVERVIEW

CHAPTER	**GUIDING QUESTIONS**
4 An interdependent learning environment for collaborative writing.	• What is an interdependent writing environment for teams? • How can I support an interdependent writing environment for teams? • How should teams structure discussions to ensure interdependent teamwork? • How can classroom activities support the values of transparency, review, and adaptation? • Which norms for teamwork, cooperation, and collaboration support interdependence? • How can a team charter help establish an interdependent writing environment for teams?
5 A writing process for interdependent collaboration.	• How do I provide meaningful feedback to teams efficiently? • How can I measure team and teammate productivity? • How should I provide feedback on collaboratively written materials? • How should teams conduct peer reviews? • How should I design a rubric for collaborative writing? • How should teammates annotate sources?
6 Create a vision for collaborative writing.	• How should I design projects for interdependent collaborative writing teams? • What are the parts of a project vision?

LIST OF TABLES

12 Table 0.1. Common obstacles to collaboration when using heuristics designed for individual writing.
16 Table 0.2. Five common roles that inspire specific tasks for writing teams.
20 Table 0.3. Collaborative writing supports development of career readiness competencies.
30 Table 1.1. Writing supports learning objectives in courses across the curriculum.
38 Table 1.2. Summary of meeting activities, agenda items, and written updates.
39 Table 1.3. Collaborative writing supports learning objectives with a combination of structural and instructional design elements.
47 Table 2.1. Learning objectives from across the curriculum intersect with five core writing objectives.
65 Table 3.1. Peer review roles named after learning objectives help immerse teams in relevant course content and writing objectives.
66 Table 3.2. Sample role-specific tasks for a writing assignment.
68 Table 3.3. Devising questions that students can use for annotating readings and drafts of team writing increases the frequency of student engagement with key objectives.
71 Table 3.4. Learning objectives, readings, and assigned writing.
73 Table 3.5. Devising objective-specific tasks helps instructors make writing expectations explicit by suggesting now only what to do but how.
84 Table 3.6. Pros and cons of various teammate role assignment approaches.
86 Table 3.7. Sample interest/confidence inventory form.
88 Table 3.8. Sample role/task board for teams.
100 Table 4.1. Pros and cons of approaches to teammate role assignment.
121 Table 5.1. Key differences between increments and drafts.
121 Table 5.2. Formative increment review complements summative peer review in interdependent writing teams.
130 Table 6.1. Collaborative writing project vision for a feasibility report. Goal is to give readers a basis for decision making.
142 Table 6.2. Sample breakdown of project grade percentage for each objective.
143 Table 6.3. Sample activities in our problem-solving framework.

LIST OF FIGURES

14 Figure 1. Values and practices in an interdependent learning environment.
15 Figure 2. Features of a collaborative writing process.
28 Figure 3. Roles and tasks for collaborative writing teams support common learning objectives across the curriculum. .
31 Figure 4. Roles that define tasks for collaborative writing.
43 Figure 5. Five concepts form the foundation of writing to learning in collaborative writing and provide direction for project design, assessment, and team productivity.
76 Figure 6. In the critical thinking role, a teammate suggests adding information about source credibility.
77 Figure 7. In the research role, a teammate reminds a collaborator to meet citation requirements.
77 Figure 8. In the genre/structure role, a teammate makes an internal comparison to promote additional content development.
78 Figure 9. A teammate in the synthesis role reminds a collaborator to indicate they have drawn their original conclusions by first consulting a valid source.
78 Figure 10. In a note on a draft report, a teammate in the review/editing role suggests an addition.
109 Figure 11. The serial writing process.
111 Figure 12. A parallel process for interdependent collaborative writing.
119 Figure 13. Reiterating consistent learning objectives during collaborative writing projects promotes deep learning.
124 Figure 14. Components of an interdependent problem-solving framework.
125 Figure 15. Associated activities in interdependent problem solving.
144 Figure 16. 5-week project sample schedule.
145 Figure 17. 10-week project sample schedule.
148 Figure 18. The *Playbook* authors: Jason Tham (left) and Joe Moses (right).

JOE

My gratitude goes out to Peter Ozolins: thank you for the unwavering love, friendship, and encouragement you've been pouring out since 1968.

To colleagues who have supported professional development in teaching (and the performing arts), thank you, Old Dogs: Angelo Volpe, James Countryman, and Timothy Gustafson.

To my daughter Katie and son Patrick: Thank you for making your lives visible to me; thank you for your honesty; and thank you for your wonderful capacity for adaptation.

Most especially, thank you to Janet Moses for your forty-two-year collaboration—for the joyful roles and the defining moments.

JASON

I am thankful for the collaborative spirit generated and shared by my peers from the University of Minnesota Emerging Technologies Research Collaboratory. Each of you played an important role in shaping this project.

To my colleagues, friends, and students at Texas Tech University, thank you for being a constant source of motivation and inspiration to me.

To friends and family members outside my immediate academic circle, thank you for being a part of my networks of care.

To Kamm, my collaborator in love and life, thank you for putting my world into meaningful, realistic perspectives. This one is for you.

ACKNOWLEDGMENTS

Thank you to our colleagues in the Department of Writing Studies at the University of Minnesota, Twin Cities (UMN), for the support and direction they have provided over recent years, including the invaluable Parlor discussions and their support of our numerous conference presentations: Ann Hill Duin, Barbara Jensen, John Logie, Lee-Ann Kastman Breuch, and Thomas Reynolds.

Thank you to the UMN Interdisciplinary Studies of Writing research program for a grant that funded our research assistant, Kendra Wiswell. We thank Kendra for her data analysis and assistance. Thank you to co-director Katie Levin for her ongoing support of our collaborative writing research through the Center for Writing.

Thank you to the UMN Writing Enriched Curriculum Program for ongoing support, and for the unit writing plans that have played a central role in our research on writing objectives for student writers: Daniel Emery, Heidi Solomonson, Matthew Lusky, Molly Bendzick, and Pamela Flash.

Thank you to members of the UMN Center for Educational Innovation for insights that contributed to our study design and evaluation: Christina Petersen, J.D. Walker, Mary Jetter, and Paul Baepler.

Thank you to members of the UMN Liberal Arts Technology Innovation Services (LATIS) who provided invaluable direction on data gathering and analysis: Thomas Lindsay, Andrew Sell, and Michael Beckstrand.

Thank you to the UMN College of Liberal Arts Interdisciplinary Collaborative Workshop Grant, funded by the Joan Aldous Innovation Fund, for supporting a year-long community of inquiry to explore collaborative writing in teaching, learning, and scholarship. Thank you to the grant team for their inspired vision for the community of inquiry: Cristina Lopez, Daniel Emery, Eduardo Nevarez, and Matthew Luskey.

And thank you to the UMN Emerging Technologies Research Collaboratory (ETRC) for demonstrating collaboration's full potential in teaching, learning, and scholarship. We thank past and current graduate student collaborators: Chakrika Veeramoothoo, Danielle Stambler, Ellen Dupler, Jeremy Rosselot-Merritt, Katlynne

ACKNOWLEDGMENTS

Davis, Nathan Bollig, Ryan Wold, and Megan McGrath; and undergraduate students Azana Adefris, Alexander Westgaard, Bilal Abdelqader, Laura Gee, Nathan Ernst, Brian Gapp, Linus Chan, John Orzechowski, and Collin Bruner.

Thank you to Jessica Chung, Curriculum & Instruction Coordinator, Leadership Minor, UMN College of Liberal Arts and to Colleen Flaherty Manchester, associate professor in the Work and Organizations department at the UMN Carlson School of Management for sharing your insights about collaborative writing and for generously contributing your teaching materials for use in the *Playbook*.

To students in our courses at the University of Minnesota and Texas Tech University, we thank them for their honesty about the obstacles they encountered while collaborating—and the creative ways they found to overcome them.

Thank you to David Blakesley at Parlor Press for his imaginative response to our initial query, and his unwavering support for our work. Thank you to Jacob Richter for his meticulous and thoughtful review of our manuscript.

To reviewers of draft chapters of the *Playbook*: thank you to Ann Hill Duin, Colleen Manchester, Eduardo Nevarez, Katie Levin, and Dan Emery for their expertise and thoughtful direction.

PREFACE

Befitting a book on collaborative writing, the *Playbook* draws from several streams of thought from writing across the curriculum, collaborative learning, design thinking, agile project management, and career readiness. Its primary purpose is to be a practical resource for instructors across disciplines who want to use writing as a mode of collaborative learning in their courses. It's for the faculty and graduate students we've met at conferences and in professional development sessions whose interests have guided our development of the *Playbook*:

> You would infuse more writing into your courses if you could invite and support team writing, so the *Playbook* includes structured activities that support teamwork and productivity.
>
> You are versed in collaborative writing, so the *Playbook* includes new ways to address challenges of trust building, accountability, motivation, and support for collaboration.
>
> You would use collaborative writing if projects produced tangible outcomes relevant to your course learning objectives, so the *Playbook* emphasizes writing activities best suited to demonstrations of learning.
>
> You are new to collaborative writing in the classroom, so the *Playbook* includes theory and research on collaboration, templates for creating effective projects and relevant writing activities that you can adapt to your courses and learning objectives.

PREFACE

Unique features of the *Playbook*

The book's purpose is to support instructors who want to include writing-to-learn opportunities for their students. With that purpose in mind, the book has several unique features:

- Practical tools for planning writing projects.
- Detailed assistance in designing writing activities so they support course learning objectives.
- A writing process that promotes productive teamwork.
- Roles for collaborative writing teammates that complement course-specific learning objectives.
- Structured activities designed specifically to support teammate interdependence and accountability.
- Formative writing assessment criteria for consistently relevant and valuable feedback from teammates and instructor.
- Tools for evaluating individual contributions to collaboratively developed content.
- Templates for team charters, team planning, goal setting, and task coordination.
- Options for ensuring writing projects demonstrate learning and application of course content in academic writing of all kinds.
- A versatile, five-part structure—defined by instructors according to their preferences—for designing and evaluating team projects. The basic structure consists of five intersections where learning and writing meet: critical thinking, research, genre/structure, synthesis, and review/editing.

INTRODUCTION

INTRODUCTION

WHY COLLABORATIVE WRITING MATTERS

INTRODUCTION

If you already include team writing projects in your courses, activities and practices from the *Playbook* can complement what you're already doing—or they might take you in new directions.

If you would include team writing in your courses if you could account for individual contributions, the *Playbook* provides relevant assessment criteria for measuring individual learning and writing achievement on collaborative writing assignments.

If you're not convinced that assigning team writing can result in equal or better individual learning outcomes than assigning individual writing, *Playbook* assessment criteria show you how to create measurable writing objectives that parallel course learning objectives, so you can decide for yourself.

If you hate team writing projects because what can go wrong does go wrong—great! So do we, because we know what can go wrong, but we have come to believe so strongly in the value of collaborative writing that we weather the wrongs to learn how they happen so we can create materials that help ourselves and others do collaborative writing right.

Finally, if you want to develop your own teaching materials for supporting writing to learn in your course, the *Playbook* gives you the tools you need. Whether writing has a central or a supporting role in your course, and whether you assign collaborative writing or projects for individuals, the *Playbook* includes resources for developing your own course text.

INTRODUCTION

Our confidence comes from our students

We believe in the value of collaborative writing because of what students say they appreciate about collaborative writing:

Learning from others during collaboration
- Understanding of different perspectives
- Improving writing by learning from peers
- Learning about topics with others

Applying collaboration outside of class
- Using the skills at work
- Using skills in other coursework
- Using skills in my individual writing

Improving my writing through collaboration
- Gaining more insight into my writing skills by working with others
- Developing my strengths
- Growing as a writer

Having positive feelings about collaborative writing
- Feeling more confident in myself
- Bringing me out of my comfort zone
- Feeling proud of our work together

Realizing advantages exclusive to team writing
- Doing something important together
- Dividing the work helped with productivity and confidence
- Having clear roles made us productive

Determining qualities of a good team
- Communicating openly
- Making strengths, weaknesses, knowledge transparent
- Dividing workload, power of collective

Realizing personal benefits of writing with others
- The pressure helping me improve
- Learning how I can benefit a team
- Gaining clarity on my strengths and weaknesses

INTRODUCTION

We've asked students who don't like team projects why they don't like team projects, and they say they hate when other team members don't do their share of the work or when they miss deadlines or when they simply disappear. They hate not knowing what teammates are working on. They hate seeing their grades fall when teammates don't hold up their end. They hate carrying the team.

Team projects are challenging—we know that. Joe, one of the authors of this book, taught writing courses for twenty years and never assigned team writing because of the outcomes of a first effort. We know from talking with other instructors that those challenges include uncertainty about evaluating individual contributions and designing and coordinating truly collaborative projects.

For all of the challenges that come with team writing, we have learned how collaborative writing can improve productivity, learning, and individual writing. We know because we have spent five years testing the ideas in this book. We have asked students to share their perspectives on collaborative writing, we have assessed the writing students have produced in teams, and we have reflected on our own engagement with students and their work.

As a result, we have identified something that's much more difficult and stressful than collaborative writing. Something more anguishing than having to share ideas with teammates or worrying about everyone making valuable contributions. Something that leads to more writing-avoidance behavior—daydreaming, binge watching, dog walking, spice-rack alphabetizing, and bathroom cleaning—than any team writing project. Something so ordinary and acceptable that people don't want to admit they would rather go to the dentist than have to bear it. Something that is also, by the way, a serious contributor to writer's block.

It's a habit we pick up in school because most schools demand it, even though in many cases it undermines student confidence.

． . . *It's writing alone.*

INTRODUCTION

Alone with dozens of questions and too much to read. Alone with fears about writing and the thoughts that gain strength as the hours that once defended against anxiety and dread become minutes:

> *I don't know how to start.*
> *Once I start, where do I finish?*
> *No matter what I write, it's not going to be good enough.*
> *I'm going to sound stupid.*
> *I waited too long to get started, and now I can't think straight.*

What's so great about writing in teams?

Writing in teams helps to silence that internal negative voice and replaces it with voices that belong neither to writer nor instructor. They're the voices that say

> *I was thinking the same thing.*
> *When can you complete that?*
> *I have an idea for you.*
> *What if we . . . ?*

We think more voices are better than one voice when it comes to writing.

INTRODUCTION

Another advantage of team writing: before students can move forward on a team project, they have to agree on what they're doing, together, which requires that they agree on what the goals are and how to reach them, so they reflect more on questions that are central to writing and critical thinking and learning: what problem are we addressing, in what way, and to what end?

The need for agreement with teammates changes almost everything about writing projects. First, it asks students to compare what they think the project is asking them to do with what others think it's asking them to do. Teammates may agree with each other's understanding, or they might understand the project differently. And voila, they're having a conversation about writing that is far richer than the solo internal monologue full of under-examined questions and under-examined answers.

> Teams give students someone besides the instructor to talk to when they have questions.

Second, teams give students someone besides the instructor to talk to when they have questions. It's not that we think asking an instructor questions is a bad idea—it's that many students tell us asking an instructor is so embarrassing that they would rather not ask. Team conversations, by contrast, often include rapid-fire questions:

When is this due, again?
Where's the link to . . . ?
How long should it be?
Are we using APA?

INTRODUCTION

It's about time

When we ask students about obstacles that get in the way of productivity, all but a handful say time management—balancing time for other courses, time for earning a paycheck, time for fun, friends, and family, with time for writing. Students also tell us that teammate commitment, support, and communication all help them improve their time management for writing.

In some cases, teammates help just by multiplying the number of reminders they deliver during meetings and in texts. That aid to memory is one way working in teams delivers productivity gains. People in teams talk a lot about what to do next, and that repetition alone helps teammates remember to complete their work. Team dynamics aid memory in additional ways—through empathy, for example. Everyone knows what counting on others feels like—how good it feels when others come through, and how good it feels to come through for others.

Writing in teams also changes everything about time: how students spend it, how they save it, invest it, borrow it, steal it, share it, and budget it. Time in college is the nonrenewable resource whose manner of consumption makes all the difference. Every student has the same amount of time to spend, save, or waste. One student has five hours to spend on a writing project. If five teammates dedicate five hours to the same project, the team invests 30 hours of intellectual energy. Teamwork multiplies the nonrenewable resource.

Teams help individuals manage time better by adding accountability to the writing process. When you tell a collaborator you're going to do something, aren't you more likely to follow through with it than if you only promise yourself? Most people, when they tell someone else they'll have work done by a certain time, want to keep their word.

INTRODUCTION

The best reasons for writing in teams

Planning with confidence

When students write alone, planning is often limited to writing a final deadline in a calendar. Not a bad place to start, but it's not really a start—it's a note about when the project is supposed to end. Writing productively requires several due dates and a plan for coordinating efforts so teammates and instructor, know whether teams are making progress long before the final due date arrives.

Valuable feedback

Teammates give each other feedback about their ideas, abilities, and writing in large and small ways while working together—from casual reminders about due dates to targeted feedback during peer review. Student feedback to us about the value of working in teams falls into four categories: the value of learning from others, of improving as a writer, of learning transfer, and of gaining confidence.

The value of learning from others: Working in teams emphasizes the social aspect of learning and often leads to increased understanding of group dynamics. More concretely, working in teams reveals to students the value that diverse contributions can make to a project. Students describe learning from others:
- Bouncing and building ideas off each other
- Clarifying by talking with teammates
- Learning that I can contribute to a team effort
- Learning new skills from others

The value of improving as a writer: Students report that teamwork benefits them individually:
- Developing my strengths
- Gaining more insight into my writing skills individually and as part of a team
- Improving my writing by seeing what teammates are doing
- Pushing me to work through boundaries

INTRODUCTION

The value of learning transfer: Students describe skills they transfer to other situations:
- Using the skills at work and in other coursework
- Document sharing helps me work more efficiently with others
- Gaining appreciation that many documents are not authored by a single person but by a team of writers
- Scrutinizing my writing more carefully inside and outside of class

The value of gaining confidence: Students report that collaborative writing results not only in collective achievement but in personal rewards:
- Feeling more confident in myself
- Bringing me out of my comfort zone
- Feeling proud of our work together
- Happily admitting my weaknesses because I know everyone has been in my shoes

Setting goals for improvement

The "freedom" of writing alone means students can set their own goals and their own timetables. Part of the freedom of writing alone comes from not having to make commitments to teammates. But writing is a commitment-driven activity. Writers have to, sooner or later, commit to exploring a topic, to testing arguments, to finding appropriate sources. The sooner they make commitments to ideas and assumptions, the sooner they can distinguish useful ideas from useless ones, accurate assumptions from wrong ones.

When students write with a team, they can check their understanding of goals with their teammates. If teammates aren't sure, individuals can approach the instructor with full confidence that they're not the only person in class who has questions.

INTRODUCTION

But what if students like writing alone?

Many students report a preference for writing alone because it's less complicated: they don't have to coordinate schedules with others or be held accountable to teammates. We propose that academic and professional writing is no different from every other kind of work students will ever have to do: it requires coordinated effort and accountability to others. In that respect, collaborative writing is more authentic than writing alone.

However, group writing projects are authentically collaborative only when they outline common goals, interdependent roles and relationships, shared resources, and measures of accountability. That is, the invitation to collaborate must be accompanied by a project design that defines and supports productive collaboration. Table 0.1 outlines common goals of authentic collaborative writing in the classroom. The writing situation includes essential elements of project design.

In many respects, students who write alone miss vital learning opportunities. How might a student's preference for writing alone limit their exposure to diverse points of view? What learning are they missing out on by not subjecting their ideas to challenges and affirmation from others?

We think the advantages of team writing far outweigh the disadvantages and that so-called disadvantages are problem-solving opportunities that add value to the writing students produce together.

Finally, writing together can help students overcome the most common obstacles that writers who work alone have to face: thinking too narrowly about what to write; being easily distracted; holding themselves to unreasonable expectations that can lead to self-doubt, false perceptions of their own ability, recurring frustration, writer's block, and missed learning opportunities.

INTRODUCTION

What's new about this *Playbook*?

The *Playbook* is the first writing guide to emphasize writers on the team as much as words on the page. Writers and words have always mattered, whether writers are working alone or in teams, but the complexities of human interaction at play in collaborative writing demand special attention. We have learned about the need for special attention through trial and error.

With respect to writing process, for example, we discovered ways in which our conception of process for collaborators included assumptions about prewriting, drafting, reviewing, and revision that didn't address realities of collaboration. When trying to achieve the positive collaborative-writing outcomes we envisioned—the sharing of multiple perspectives among teammates, the taking advantage of teammate strengths, to name two of many—without modifying the writing process, we met with several obstacles we hadn't encountered when designing projects for individuals to complete alone.

When addressing instruction to individual writers, we used the four-part process heuristic—Prewriting | Drafting | Review | Revision—employing a recursive process of low-stakes writing activities, higher-stakes drafts, students giving and receiving a peer review, and receiving instructor feedback, followed by revisions of work to turn in for a grade. At every step, we encountered obstacles.

Table 0.1. **Common obstacles to collaboration when using heuristics designed for individual writing.**

Heuristics for writers working alone	Obstacle to collaborative writers
Prewriting: freewriting, brainstorming to engage individual writers with a topic.	Diverse engagement. Wide-ranging interests, experience, and understanding of the topic.
Drafting: researching to develop content relevant to a student's topic and purpose, research question, and hypothesis.	An imperative of expediency: the impulse among students to make hasty decisions, often based on ideas expressed by the most vocal teammate(s).
Review of drafts: response guidelines for student pairs, for feedback after extensive drafting..	Redundant responses provided late in the assignment schedule.
Revision: editing in response to peer and instructor review comments.	Insufficient familiarity with project requirements as the deadline approaches.

New directions for team writing

The concept of cross-functional teams, adopted from an agile project management framework, prompted us to test a new heuristic for team writing—one that would accurately reflect realities of collaboration and suggest the complexity of collaboration without overwhelming students. In agile project management, teams include members who have different areas of expertise. They work together in parallel to meet project requirements for a small part of the whole project. Working together on the small parts, or increments, raises questions—about purpose, for example—that inform decision-making while working on subsequent increments. Discussed in greater detail in chapter 5, a similar process modified specifically for writing teams creates opportunities for interaction that address the obstacles we outline above.

The new based on the familiar

Although new in some respects, our interdependent, project-based model has several features in common with familiar individual-based process models—differing significantly, however, in purpose.

INTRODUCTION

The *Playbook*'s emphasis on time, tasks, and course learning objectives may be its most radical departure from other team writing textbooks. Anyone who has worked to complete a writing assignment by a deadline already knows the importance of time, but the *Playbook* emphasizes time more persistently than other approaches.

How students manage their time, how they save it, spend it, estimate it, allot it, and waste it all have a bearing on the value of the writing that teams and individuals produce—and on the writing experience for everyone who participates. Time is the most valuable nonrenewable resource in a student's life, so when we ask students about the most pressing obstacle to productivity, they most commonly responded, "Time!" By emphasizing time, we have set out to help students reimagine time as a resource instead of an obstacle. Time and the alignment of writing with learning objectives helps make teammates more productive.

Tasks—what students do, and why and when, should always be top of mind, but how students conceive of tasks and their priority is an especially powerful factor in team success. Which writing tasks should I complete and which ones should I complete first?

Course learning objectives—the central driver of course content—must also drive the design of writing assignments. The *Playbook* takes readers through a step-by-step process of aligning writing-as-a-mode-of-learning with course-specific content, modes of inquiry, and learning outcomes.

Twenty-first century writing assignments that strive only to challenge students to demonstrate knowledge through individual expressions of their own thinking insufficiently prepare students for communication challenges in the organizations they will enter upon graduation. As communication channels and tools multiply, so do the challenges of learning quickly enough. An emphasis on learning in writing teams instead of individual learning for individual writing is therefore central to educational missions across the curriculum.

INTRODUCTION

New: An interdependent learning environment

Chapter 4 details the elements of an interdependent learning environment that supports collaborative writing as a mode of engagement with course content. Drawn from agile project management practices, the elements of an interdependent learning environment emphasize values outlined above. How instructors introduce, model, and sustain values that support their learning objectives may vary significantly in disciplines as different from each other as computer science and theater. Nevertheless, we propose three values that help sustain interdependent collaboration: transparency, frequent review, and adaptation.

- **Transparency:** Enabling students to make thinking—and learning—visible; making instructor thinking and learning visible.
- **Review:** Accommodating frequent discussions about content that teams and teammates develop.
- **Adaptation:** Welcoming change based on 1) what students learn about each other and their project—and 2) what instructors learn about students.

An environment that supports interdependent writing and learning when classroom time reinforces three values and practices:

VALUES	PRACTICES
Transparency	Making thinking visible
Review	Brief, frequent presentations about achievement
Adaptation	Changing behavior based on learning

Figure 1. **Values and practices in an interdependent learning environment.**

INTRODUCTION

New: A collaborative writing process

When conducted in an environment of transparency, inspection, and adaptation, a collaborative writing process supports productivity and learning by building trust among teammates. A collaborative writing process focuses on writers on a team as well as writing on the page.

EMPATHIZING	Activities for understanding thoughts and feelings of readers, teammates, and instructor
DEFINING	Activities for defining project terms, problems, and constraints.
PROTOTYPING	Activities for generating multiple solutions.
INCREMENT REVIEW	Activities for discussing how increments do and do not meet project requirements.
TEAM RETROSPECTIVE	Activities for reflecting as a team on the effectiveness of their practices, and to make continuous improvements.

Figure 2. **Features of a collaborative writing process.**

INTRODUCTION

New: interdependent roles for teammates

Roles for students in writing teams should be distinctive but familiar, so we base teammate roles on common writing activities that align with course learning objectives. We know our basic roles align with learning objectives across the curriculum because we have compared the roles with Writing Enriched Curriculum writing plans produced by faculty from across the curriculum in which instructors characterize writing in their disciplines and writing abilities they value in their students.

While the roles do align with many learning objectives across the curriculum, they are not meant to be exhaustive or exclusive; they are instead a place to start when reflecting on the role of writing in any course.

Table 0.2. **Five common roles that inspire specific tasks for writing teams.**

Basic roles	Task categories for interdependent writing teams
Critical thinking	Course-specific evaluation and interpretation tasks
Research	Tasks related to modes of inquiry in a discipline
Genre/Structure	Tasks for meeting genre expectations and proper organization
Synthesis	Tasks for applying course content
Review/Editing	Tasks for peer and instructor review and revision based on course standards

INTRODUCTION

New: Templates that support efficiency

The *Playbook* includes:

- Templates for
  » Project visions
  » Collaborative writing activities
  » Team review sessions
  » Team retrospectives about productivity
  » Project-specific design-thinking activities
  » Continuous improvement survey for teams
  » Editing checklists
  » Interest/confidence inventory for teammate relationship building
  » Team update memos for task coordination
  » Team retrospective memos for goal setting
- Annotation guides for demonstrating knowledge about assigned readings or sources
- Peer review guides that promote interdependent writing

INTRODUCTION

Origins

The *Playbook* draws on four intersections of work and learning: design thinking, team-based working and learning, agile project management methods, and career readiness.

Design thinking for words on the page and writers on the team

Design thinking has emerged as a valuable heuristic for managing the complexities of writing and instruction. Richard Marback (2009) aligns the value of design thinking with its engagement of participants with "problems of responsiveness that are interpretive as well as affective" (p. W400). That is, design thinking accommodates the critical thinking objectives of academic coursework to the emotional work of collaborative problem-solving. Advancing Marback's argument, James Purdy (2014) aligns the value of design thinking with its engagement of participants in collaboration (p. 633). To support production of words on the page and writers on a team, we outline practices that ask teammates to pay attention to important interpersonal dimensions of writing.

Team-based working and learning

Organizations are doing more than paying lip service to the idea of teamwork. Researcher at Stanford University report that just the feeling of working together motivates people to work "48–64% longer on a challenging task . . . reported greater interest in the task . . . required less self-regulatory resources to persist on it . . . became more engrossed in the task and performed better on it . . . and spontaneously expressed greater enjoyment of and interest in the task" (Carr & Walton, 2014, p. 181).

INTRODUCTION

In their analysis of 1,000 technical communication job postings, Eva Brumberger and Claire Lauer concluded that collaboration and time management ranked as the highest-valued personal characteristics of candidates (2015, p. 237). Teamwork is a strong and persistent value in business and in higher education, and the *Playbook* is designed to provide students with valuable experience that increases their learning in college while preparing them for team-based working. Deloitte's Human Capital Trends 2018 puts a fine point on the demand for teamwork extending far beyond the academy: "As the business environment becomes more competitive and digital disruption continues, organizations have become more team-centric, networked, and agile" (p. 17).

Deloitte's analysis follows on the same trend they identified in the 2016 edition of Human Capital Trends in which they noted that "A new organizational model is on the rise: a 'network of teams' in which companies build and empower teams to work on specific business projects and challenges" (n.p.).

Agile methods that support productive teamwork

Researchers have identified project management principles that add value to writing instruction (Pope-Ruark, 2012, 2015; Moses, 2015). Stanley Dicks (2013) advocates for explicit instructional practices that make project management expectations apparent and team working processes transparent to make team projects more meaningful and productive for students. Rebecca Pope-Ruark has also tested the agile principle of making working processes transparent to improve team-writing experience (2012, 2015). Research investigating roles in team-based learning describes the importance of assigned roles in team learning (Johnson, Johnson, & Smith, 2007), and the value of positive interdependence (Brewer & Klein, 2006) as keys to advancing writing and learning in teams. We have adapted elements of agile project management to the purposes of writing-to-learn in teams.

INTRODUCTION

Collaborative writing supports career readiness

As the National Association of Colleges and Employers define it, "Career readiness is the attainment and demonstration of requisite competencies that broadly prepare college graduates for a successful transition into the workplace" (NACE). Table 0.3 outlines some of the ways collaborative writing can support key career readiness competencies.

Table 0.3. **Collaborative writing supports development of career readiness competencies.**

Career readiness competencies	Collaborative writing practices
Analytical & Critical Thinking	Conducting research together, comparing interpretations of information.
Applied Problem Solving	Working together to solve writing problems.
Ethical Reasoning & Decision Making	Teammates make ethical decisions regarding their audiences and their teammates.
Innovation & Creativity	Teammates challenge each other with new ideas and approaches to productivity.
Oral & Written Communication	Teammates hold each other accountable to high standards for clarity and accuracy.
Teamwork & Leadership	Teamwork immerses students in collaboration and cooperation.
Engaging Diversity	Students engage with diverse teammates.
Digital Literacy	Teammates practice using a variety of tools: shared documents, content management systems, communication technologies.

Chapters synopsis

Chapter 1: What does a good collaborative writing project look like?

The key to strong collaboration is the creation of teammate roles based directly on learning objectives. Because roles serve a collective goal while focusing individual attention to specific project features, we call the roles interdependent. In interdependent roles, teammates perform different but complementary tasks.

Chapter 2: How can collaborative writing support your course learning objectives?

We introduce five basic roles and categories of tasks, such as research and critical thinking, and provide a step-by-step process for aligning collaborative writing projects with course learning objectives.

Chapter 3: Collaborative writing roles and tasks for interdependent teamwork

Because tasks and roles vary widely by course, instructor, and department, no single set of tasks can meet every learning objective. We detail five basic roles as models and a guide to modifying the roles or creating new roles to serve your course. The five basic roles for individuals on writing teams include research, critical thinking, genre (or structuring), synthesizing ideas, and reviewing/editing. With those basic roles in mind, Chapter 3 outlines a process for customizing roles and tasks according to course learning objectives.

Chapter 4: An interdependent learning environment for collaborative writing

No team is automatically productive. Teams need a shared understanding of goals, structure, roles, and tasks plus an agreement about how teammates will work together. To support goal sharing, Chapter 4 includes practical ideas and activities for creating timely, professional, and clear communications, for seeking positive team outcomes, for helping teammates take on unfamiliar tasks, and for positively influencing the team during challenges.

Chapter 5: A writing process for interdependent collaboration

We draw on four themes that have emerged since the turn of the 21st century to place interdependent collaboration at the center of the writing process: the increasingly acknowledged value of team-based working and learning—especially in the value of positive interdependence (Johnson & Johnson, 2007) in collaborative learning; the emergence of agile frameworks for project teams, the effectiveness of design thinking as a driver of innovation, and the emphasis on career readiness in higher education. Based on those themes, we outline a collaborative writing process for courses across the curriculum at the intersection of instructional design discipline (writing-to-learning via positive interdependence), a problem-solving discipline (design thinking) and a project management discipline (agile). When combined with teammate roles based on course learning objectives, a writing process for authentic interdependence makes the complexities of writing both visible and manageable through collaboration.

Chapter 6: Create a vision for collaborative writing

The purpose of a project vision is to provide teams with a reference that guides learning throughout the project. Like familiar assignment sheets, the vision outlines project goals and purpose, with grading criteria and other important details. Perhaps unlike familiar assignment sheets, the vision also discusses teammate tasks and roles and how they align with course learning objectives. The calendar explains how often teammates will be able to use class time for planning, reviewing teammate work, and working to improve team processes. When collaborative writing isn't suited to a project, teammates can still provide valuable feedback, so the chapter includes a vision template for individual writing and collaborative peer review.

INTRODUCTION

A note on the five basic writing objectives

Readers may notice that we come back to five basic writing objectives throughout the *Playbook*: critical thinking, research, genre/structure, synthesis, and review/editing. We come back to them for two key reasons—one empirical and one theoretical.

As we discuss in chapter 2, we have observed from analysis of faculty writing plans for the Writing Enriched Curriculum Program at the University of Minnesota that the five basic writing objectives accurately reflect faculty objectives for students writing in fields as diverse as women's studies, biological science, Spanish/Portuguese studies, theater and dance, African American studies, and business. That is, the objectives are essential to any approach to writing, across the curriculum. As basic objectives, they are also subject to innumerable interpretations and applications—and revisions—according to readers' understanding of writing to learn in their courses and fields.

The theoretical basis for coming back to the five writing objectives throughout the *Playbook* comes from a principle of learning in *How Learning Works: Seven Research-Based Principles for Smart Teaching*:

> Goal-directed practice coupled with targeted feedback enhances the quality of students' learning.
>
> Learning and performance are best fostered when students engage in practice that focuses on a specific goal or criterion, targets an appropriate level of challenge, and is of sufficient quantity and frequency to meet the performance criteria. Practice must be coupled with feedback that explicitly communicates about some aspect(s) of students' performance relative to specific target criteria, provides information to help students progress in meeting those criteria, and is given at a time and frequency that allows it to be useful. (Ambrose et al., 2010, p. 6)

INTRODUCTION

As performance criteria, the five basic writing objectives provide a framework for targeted feedback with a frequency that enhances the quality of student learning.

- Most course content—readings, lectures, activities, assignments—illustrates modes of critical thinking, research, genre/structure, synthesis, and professional publishing standards (the result of review and editing).
- Readings that support course-specific learning objectives are also typically discipline-specific models of critical thinking, research, genre/structure, synthesis, and professional publishing standards.
- Lectures embody disciplinary modes of critical thinking, research, genre/structure, synthesis, and professional publishing standards (the result of review and editing).
- Activities engage students in practices whose processes and outcomes are typically inscribed according to discipline-specific guidelines for the five writing objectives.
- Assignments, including writing assignments, test student achievement in critical thinking, research, genre/structure, synthesis, and review/editing according to professional publishing standards.

When instructors align the five writing objectives with course learning objectives, they can take full advantage of writing to learn in courses across the curriculum.

CHAPTER 1

WHAT DOES A GOOD COLLABORATIVE WRITING PROJECT LOOK LIKE?

GUIDING QUESTIONS

- What is collaborative writing?
- How can collaborative writing support course learning objectives?
- What are structured activities?
- How can teams make meetings productive?

CHAPTER 1

Lisa Ede and Andrea Lunsford have set the stage for contemporary thinking about collaborative writing in their examination of collaborative authoring in the workplace, where they identified sources of job satisfaction among individuals who write collaboratively:

- the degree to which goals are articulated and shared;
- the degree of openness and mutual respect;
- the degree of control the writers have over the text;
- the degree to which writers can respond to others who modify the text;
- the way in which credit (directly or indirectly) is acknowledged;
- the presence of an agreed upon procedure for managing conflicts and resolving disputes;
- the number and types of (bureaucratic) constraints imposed on the authors—deadlines, technical/legal requirements, etc., and;
- the status of the project within the organization (1990, p. 65).

We have found Ede and Lunsford's sources useful when designing a collaborative writing environment for student teams because they have helped us identify and address obstacles to team productivity that surface during projects.

The literature on collaborative writing roles, whether in academic or nonacademic settings, is similarly helpful in providing direction when designing effective collaborative writing projects, especially when discussions employ "role" terminology that is descriptive of writing tasks—writer, editor, reviewer, scribe (Lowry, Curtis, & Lowry, 2004, p. 86), or "writer, researcher, editor, and typist" (Page & Donelan, 2003 p. 128).

CHAPTER 1

While such roles do name some valuable attitudes and activities for collaborative writing, they can also dilute the potential of collaboration through arbitrariness and lack of definition. As Rebecca E. Burnett, Christianna I. White, and Ann Hill Duin (1997) argue, students advance beyond mere interaction to true collaboration when their efforts share "intentionality and purpose" (p. 137).

We have found some roles for collaborative writing teammates to be less effective, including the frequently recurring advice about team roles that, while reflecting research on small-group dynamics, do not fully align writing practices with learning objectives: roles that emerge during projects, such as mentor, social performer, independent writer, and help-seeking writer (Nordmark, 2017); team-process roles designed to foster interdependence, such as reader, checker, and encourager (Johnson, Johnson, & Smith, 1991); and with classroom teammate roles of captain, recorder, reflector, spokesperson, technology specialist, planner, timekeeper, skeptic, optimist, and spy (Smith & Krumsieg, 2003).

The *Playbook* departs from roles based on small-group dynamics to focus on teammate roles that align with course learning objectives. Roles, learning objectives, and alignment are the basis for the definition of collaborative writing in higher education that we use throughout the *Playbook*.

> **The *Playbook* definition of interdependent collaborative writing**
>
> Structured activities for teammates in writing roles that complement course-specific learning objectives.

CHAPTER 1

Structured activities
Team update meetings
Team review sessions
Team retrospective discussions
Update memos for team coordination
Team charter activity
Team interest/confidence survey

for teammates in writing roles
Roles define specific tasks to perform while writing and during peer review.

that complement course-specific learning objectives
Five key writing roles and tasks support course-specific learning objectives:

Learning objectives	Roles and writing tasks
Conveying what course content means.	Critical thinking
Contextualizing course content.	Research
Organizing knowledge appropriately.	Genre/structure
Applying course content.	Synthesis
Presenting knowledge according to disciplinary standards.	Review/editing

Figure 3. **Roles and tasks for collaborative writing teams support common learning objectives across the curriculum.**

CHAPTER 1

Align writing requirements with course-specific learning objectives.

Course learning objectives are the best guide to goal-setting for collaborative writing projects because they identify common ground shared by writing, learning, and disciplinary practice.

In courses across the curriculum, instructors name learning objectives that align directly with measurable achievements in student writing (see WEC Writing Plans). As the examples of learning objectives from diverse fields illustrate (Table 1.1), writing supports learning objectives for critical thinking, problem-solving, genre-based modes of analysis and synthesis, and professional publication standards.

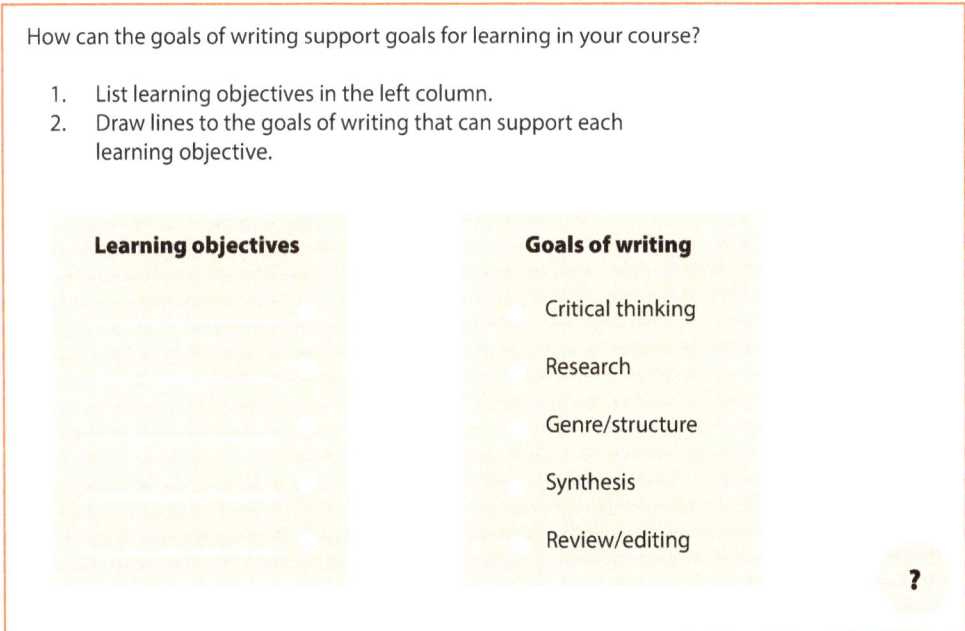

How can the goals of writing support goals for learning in your course?

1. List learning objectives in the left column.
2. Draw lines to the goals of writing that can support each learning objective.

Learning objectives

Goals of writing

Critical thinking

Research

Genre/structure

Synthesis

Review/editing

CHAPTER 1

Table 1.1. **Writing supports learning objectives in courses across the curriculum.**

Discipline	Learning objectives	How writing supports learning objectives
Nursing	Use critical thinking skills in delivery of patient-centered care.	Writing is inherently a critical thinking activity.
Mechanical Engineering	Identify, formulate, and solve engineering problems.	Writing is a problem-solving activity reflecting modes of inquiry valued by disciplines.
Geology	Demonstrate competence in quantitative data analysis.	Writing is a common method in higher education for demonstrating competence in research and analysis.
Drama and Dance	Analyze historical movements in dramatic literature and practice.	Writing is a mode of analysis across disciplines, with written genres helping to guide the form that analyses and synthesis should take.
Political Science	Identify questions germane to the study and practice of politics and explain their relevance; synthesize and evaluate existing approaches to these questions by highlighting their strengths and weaknesses.	Synthesis, or combining, interpreting, and evaluating information from multiple sources, is a nearly universal objective in courses across the curriculum, most frequently demonstrated through writing.
Technical Communication	Revise and edit your work and that of your classmates so that your writing is stylistically appropriate and grammatically correct.	All disciplines have publication guidelines that emphasize professional standards.

CHAPTER 1

Align teammate roles with writing requirements.

The second part of the collaborative writing definition refers to the need for well-defined roles for teammates. Roles and associated tasks should give teammates direction while writing and focus during peer review. Roles and tasks should outline goals and learning objectives of the entire project.

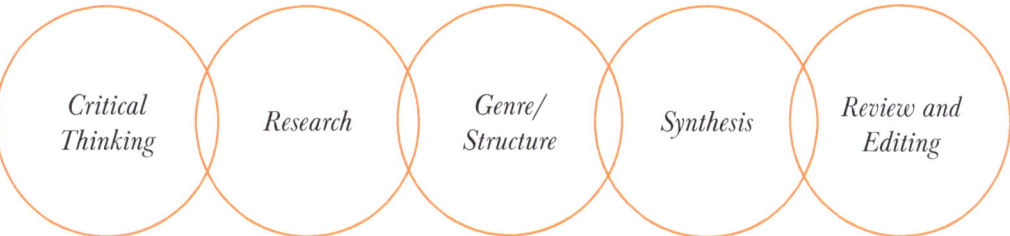

Figure 4. **Roles that define tasks for collaborative writing.**

We use an expansive definition of writing to include types of inscription for visual as well as textual communication. Similarly, while we refer to documents throughout the *Playbook*, we recognize that instructors may assign digital media projects and information development for blogs, podcasts, virtual or augmented reality, video, and other media. We will use the shorthand of "writing" and "documents" throughout the *Playbook* and ask those terms to stand in for the terminology you bring to your courses.

CHAPTER 1

Include structured activities that support interdependent collaboration.

By structure we mean reliable, repeatable activities designed to support interdependent collaboration:

- Synchronous writing activities
- Productivity measures (word counts, time spent)
- Conversations about collaborative writing
- Conversations about team productivity
- Evaluation of team writing
- Team meetings for updates and accountability
- Team-written updates on writing and productivity

Synchronous writing activities

When teammates can write together at the same time, they get to see what their teammates are thinking—and so do instructors. Short, simple activities give teammates insights into their teammates' ways of thinking and styles of writing.

CHAPTER 1

Productivity measures (word counts, time spent)

While so much of productivity can be attributed to factors that are hard to measure—attitudes toward teamwork, commitment to common goals, for two examples—asking students to make concrete commitments to measurable goals is an effective practice for instructors and a reassuring one for student teams. Under the pressures from work, family, and other courses that compete for students' time, teammates may give vague responses to questions about how they plan to contribute to team projects. "I'm going to write on Saturday," "I'll work on it tomorrow," "I'll annotate two sources by Thursday," or "I'll write two-hundred words on topic X for your review by 9 tonight," and you can see the difference that productivity measures can make. Good collaborative writing projects give students guidelines for reporting their efforts so instructors and teammates can tell whether teams are making adequate progress.

Conversations about collaborative writing

In Chapter 5 we detail a process for authentic collaboration that includes time for reflecting, as a team, on teamwork, cooperation, collaboration, and communicating outside of class. Such conversations are not incidental to course objectives; rather, they are integral to problem-solving as teams pursue course learning objectives.

CHAPTER 1

Conversations about team productivity

Giving teams a chance to reflect on what's working and what's not helps teams identify obstacles and how to overcome them. Chapter 5 includes a team retrospective activity that focuses team conversations about their productivity and how to improve it.

> In your experience, what are the characteristics of a productive student team?

Evaluation of team writing

Chapter 5 details a writing process that includes an activity called team review during which 1) teams present small parts, or increments, of a project and discuss how increments meet learning objectives, and 2) instructor and other teams provide timely feedback.

CHAPTER 1

Team meetings for updates and accountability

Team meetings and productivity go hand-in-hand. Whether meetings take place in class or outside of class, meetings give students a chance to check in with each other about what they're doing and why.

1. Team update meetings

Teams should hold several update meetings per week. Lasting only fifteen minutes at most, update meetings are informal discussions in which all teammates respond to three questions:

1. What have you completed since the last meeting?
2. What do you plan to complete by the next meeting?
3. What obstacles to productivity are you encountering?

A few ground rules help ensure that update meetings are productive:

- All teammates take a turn to answer the questions.
- No phones or other personal devices in use; meeting times are not bathroom or snack breaks.
- All teammates are encouraged to be present.
- Teammates collaboratively write a team update memo after everyone has spoken.
- Team update memos about tasks completed or to be completed should be concrete and quantifiable: not "I wrote some stuff, but "I wrote 200 words on the topic of _____; I read eight pages of _____; I spent two hours researching the question of _____."
- A teammate is assigned or volunteers to notify absent teammates of the update memo activity requirements.

CHAPTER 1

2. Team review meetings

Team review is an informal presentation of an increment of work that teams have developed. Increments that teams select for review should be brief. An increment is any kind of content that teams have created to meet project requirements: words, titles, images, sentences, headings, or paragraphs.

Each teammate should discuss how the increment addresses specific objectives of the project. For example, an instructor using the five basic requirement/role categories of critical thinking, research, genre/structure, synthesis, and review/editing, would ask students to discuss how an increment of their team's work meets requirements for each role. During team review, teams receive feedback and have a chance to compare their project with other teams' work. Team review meetings don't have to be long to be effective, but at minimum, teams should describe ways the increment meets or attempts to meet project requirements.

Purpose of team review: Students convey their current understanding of project requirements by presenting an increment of writing they consider to be finished.

Length of team review presentation: 5-10 minutes

In the space below, make a list of increments you consider valid for this activity (images, titles, paragraphs, captions, for example).

Valid increments could be:

CHAPTER 1

3. Team retrospective meetings

Frequent retrospectives give teammates a chance to discuss what's working in their teams, what's not working, and how to change what they're going to do during the next working period.

Retrospectives have three components: 1) a continuous improvement update, 2) a team retrospective meeting, and 3) a retrospective update memo. Together, the retrospective activities set a direction for improving team productivity.

Continuous improvement update
To prepare for team retrospectives, complete the following survey of teammate participation. Using the teammate continuous improvement update gives you a chance to improve team and individual productivity prior to evaluation by your instructor. The process also helps you compare understandings of key objectives for your team and reach consensus about your objectives. See Chapter 5 for a survey model.

Team retrospective meeting
During retrospectives, teammates discuss their perspectives on three questions.

- What has been working well?
- What hasn't been working well?
- What can the team do differently right away to improve productivity?

Retrospective update memo
Co-authoring the update memo ensures that everyone's perspectives are included.

Meeting summary

Table 1.2. **Summary of meeting activities, agenda items, and written updates.**

Meeting activities	Agenda	Team-written updates
Team update 15 minutes, max. Daily or as often as possible.	Tasks update Time spent, tasks completion % What's finished? What will you complete by the next meeting? What obstacles have you encountered? What obstacles do you anticipate encountering? How will you work at overcoming obstacles?	**Team update memo**
Team review 15 minutes, max. Every two weeks or as needed.	**What to prepare:** Pull up a Google doc with your increment. Make sure everyone on your team can access it. An increment is any written work that you consider finished, so it may be words, phrases, sentences, titles, a definition, research question, thesis, subtitle, outline, single paragraph, or any other content large or small. **What to discuss:** each teammate takes turns explaining their increment(s) from the point of view of a specific role/requirement. Teammates listen and respond with follow up questions.	**Team review memo** including a summary of what they plan to do next based on the feedback they've received
Team retrospective 15 minutes, max. Twice per project or as needed.	What has been working well? What hasn't been working well? What will you do differently right away?	**Teammate continuous improvement update** **Team retrospective memo**

Collaborative writing and structure

The structural elements of collaborative writing can support a variety of instructional designs. Table 1.3 outlines the elements we emphasize in the *Playbook*.

Table 1.3. **Collaborative writing supports learning objectives with a combination of structural and instructional design elements.**

Structural elements	Instructional design elements
Learning objectives	• Critical thinking goals • Research goals • Genre/structure goals • Synthesis goals • Review/editing (professional publishing standards) goals
Teammate roles and tasks	• Critical thinking tasks • Research tasks • Genre/structure tasks • Synthesis tasks • Review/editing (professional publishing standards) tasks
Team meetings	• Team review: Frequent, brief presentations of team direction and written increments • Team updates and memos: periodic teammate check-in. What have you completed, what will you complete, what obstacles do you anticipate? • Team retrospectives: what is working in your team, what isn't working, what will you do differently right away to improve productivity?
The environment	• Making thinking visible • Using shared documents for ease of collaboration • Classroom activities that support interdependent collaboration
The writing process	• Empathizing with audiences and teammates • Problem definition • Prototyping: drafting, outlining, increment development • Increment review: receiving frequent, brief feedback on increments and team direction • Team retrospectives: reviewing and improving team productivity
Activities and assignments	• Models of effective writing in the discipline • Models of past student writing • Examples of effective critical thinking • Examples of research • Models of genre/structure • Models of synthesis • Models of review/editing; interdependent peer review • Discussion practice

CHAPTER 2

HOW CAN COLLABORATIVE WRITING SUPPORT YOUR COURSE LEARNING OBJECTIVES?

GUIDING QUESTIONS

- Where does collaborative writing intersect with course learning objectives?
- What are my course objectives for critical thinking?
- What are my course objectives for research?
- What are my course objectives for genre/structure?
- What are my course objectives for synthesis?
- What are my course objectives for review/editing?

CHAPTER 2

Assigning collaborative writing can lead to significant reduction in time you spend on repetitious feedback to students about their work. Because you can address responses to a team of six, for example, instead of six individual students, you work more efficiently. As importantly, your comments to six students are subject to multiple interpretations that promote teammate discussions, and those discussions promote learning.

But feedback can vary dramatically in value, whether it's delivered to individuals or to teams. The key to efficient and valuable feedback is to align writing objectives with course learning objectives. Aligning your feedback with key learning objectives simplifies response—and evaluation—while multiplying the impact of the time you spend on a vital teaching activity. Your targeted responses also make students' collaborative writing efforts more productive because each suggestion you make for improvement serves relevant, high-priority learning objectives for your course.

Where does writing intersect with course learning objectives?

Instructors who want to use writing as a mode of learning can use five familiar concepts in genres across the curriculum. The five concepts provide a rigorous yet flexible framework for designing projects, assessing student work, and guiding productive collaborations among teammates.

CHAPTER 2

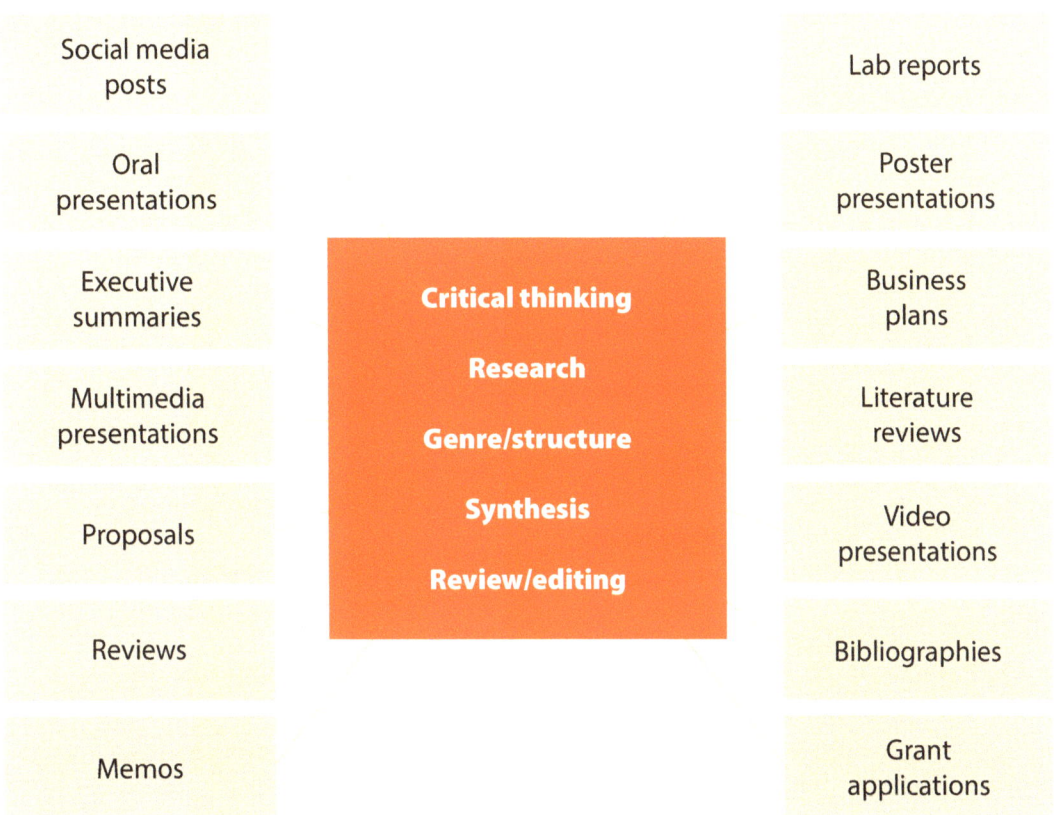

Figure 5. **Five concepts form the foundation of writing to learning in collaborative writing and provide direction for project design, assessment, and team productivity.**

CHAPTER 2

Throughout the *Playbook*, we use the same five intersections of writing and learning, outlined below, as a starting point for reflecting on the role of writing to learn in your courses.

- **Critical thinking:** In STEM fields, activities include using knowledge and skills in problem solving. In arts and humanities courses, activities are often defined in visual, rhetorical, or analytical terms for identifying in course materials and achieving in students' written work effective strategies for interpreting and evaluating information.
- **Research:** Activities for achieving course-specific research objectives for information gathering.
- **Genre/structure:** Activities for demonstrating course-specific knowledge of genre guidelines for relevant content, organization, and formatting.
- **Synthesis:** Activities for course-specific achievement in integrating source material, applying theories, and generating original insights in discipline-appropriate ways.
- **Review/editing:** Activities for discipline-specific achievement in preparing final materials for evaluation and publication.

Assigning activities that correspond to the five learning objectives sets the stage for productive team writing and learning. As we discuss throughout the *Playbook*, the intersections also provide guidelines for content development, content analysis, and peer review in course-specific ways.

If you already have a list of learning objectives for your course, some of your work is already complete. If not, the following section outlines a process for crafting learning objectives for your course.

CHAPTER 2

Step 1: Outline course learning objectives

Step 2: Outline critical thinkings objectives

Step 3: Determine high-priority researching objectives

Step 4: Introduce students to genre/structure objectives

Step 5: Define synthesis objectives

Step 6: Introduce students to review/editing objectives

CHAPTER 2

Step 1: Outline course learning objectives

While learning objectives vary widely by course and program, instructors can draw from several common sources of learning objectives without having to start from scratch:

- Course, Program, College learning objectives
- Common margin notes to students
- Instructor's teaching objectives
- Instructor's teaching values
- Instructor's existing rubrics
- Unit writing plans (programmatic writing goals by major). See examples in Tables 1.1 and 2.1.
- Instructor's teaching journal

Table 2.1 illustrates intersections of course learning objectives from across the curriculum, with the five basic writing objectives we outlined previously. We have indicated where each learning objective aligns explicitly with writing objectives. For example, "Use critical thinking skills in delivery of effective patient-centered care (Nursing)" explicitly names critical thinking as an objective. In some cases, the intersections are implicit, as in the Accounting example, which suggests to us objectives for meeting genre requirements and ensuring accuracy via review/editing tasks.

CHAPTER 2

Table 2.1. **Learning objectives from across the curriculum intersect with five core writing objectives.**

Learning objective samples	Objectives aligned with writing				
	Critical thinking	Research	Genre/ Structure	Synthesis	Review/ Editing
Use critical thinking skills in delivery of effective patient-centered care (Nursing).	✓				
Identify, formulate, and effectively solve engineering problems (Mechanical Engineering).	✓				
Demonstrate competence in accurate, relevant quantitative data analysis (Geology)		✓			
Critically analyze historical movements in dramatic literature and practice (Drama and Dance)		✓			
Communicate financial information by producing and processing accurate financial statements (Accounting).			✓		✓
Identify and apply the objectives involved in Total Quality Management (Business).				✓	

CHAPTER 2

Step 2: Outline your critical thinking objectives

Expectations for critical thinking vary widely by discipline, course, major, and instructor. Orienting students to the critical thinking abilities you value in your course not only helps to focus student attention when writing but can guide strategies for analyzing course readings. Arriving at five or more critical thinking objectives helps students see a variety of ways to meet critical thinking objectives and reveals the complexity of critical thinking in your field.

Making your expectations for critical thinking explicit aids course-specific student learning because faculty definitions of critical thinking vary widely. The manner in which faculty describe critical thinking objectives also varies, as the following examples demonstrate:

- Demonstrate understanding of the matrix of domination and strategies for resistance to domination (African American and African Studies).
- Convey information at appropriate levels of scientific sophistication based on target audience (Horticultural Science).
- Distance personal biases from the data (Agronomy).
- To demonstrate an understanding of target philosophers' ideas through effective paraphrase and argument reconstruction rather than merely relying on quotation (Philosophy).
- Develop an interpretation of a cultural, literary, or linguistic object of study (Spanish).

CHAPTER 2

Outline the high-priority critical thinking objectives for your course

Students who master critical thinking skills for my course should be able to:

1.
2.
3.
4.
5.

?

Model transparency

For each critical thinking objectives you want students to pursue, provide models to show students what the objective looks like in your field. Using the five examples listed above, models might include:

- Sample paraphrases in readings or past student work that show accurate interpretation of a relevant theory.
- Samples that convey information at appropriate levels of scientific sophistication based on a target audience.
- Incorrect and correct models of distancing bias from data.
- Models of effective and ineffective paraphrases and argument reconstructions.
- Models of valid interpretations of cultural, literary, or linguistic objects of study.

CHAPTER 2

Schedule brief reviews of student work

For each critical thinking objective you want students to pursue, schedule time for criterion-based conversations about student achievement in their writing:

- Where does the work accurately/inaccurately paraphrase course content?
- Where does the work achieve appropriate levels of scientific sophistication; where does it not?
- Where does the work appropriately represent data without bias; where does it not?
- Where does the work effectively paraphrase or reconstruct arguments; where does it not?
- Where does the work include valid interpretations; where does it not?

Give students tools for adapting based on what they learn during reviews

Assign teams to add critical thinking reminders to their individual editing checklists, including your expectations for audience, purpose, and definition.

Personal editing checklists: instruct student to add critical thinking strategies to their checklists after each review, such as:

- Paraphrase more selectively.
- Remember to use appropriate vocabulary.
- Check graph scales to avoid misrepresenting data.
- Remember to capture all key ideas in paraphrases; express key arguments in your own words.
- Review interpretations with teammates.

CHAPTER 2

Step 3: Determine high-priority researching objectives

Because research practices, genres, and purposes vary by discipline, orienting students to the research objectives for your course helps to focus student attention on high-value practices.

Getting started

Outline research objectives you have for students in your course. Arriving at five or more researching objectives helps students see a variety of ways to meet objectives and reveals the complexity of research in your field.

Faculty expectations for research vary widely, as the following examples demonstrate:

- Formulate research or thesis questions that are appropriate in scope and topic (College of Biological Sciences).
- Define hypotheses in order to clarify the purpose of the work (Chemistry).
- Use effective, valid data/evidence that is relevant to audience concerns (Carlson School of Management).
- Gather ideas drawn from a variety of sources (Design, Housing, and Apparel).
- Formulate viable historical research questions and hypotheses, and express these effectively in written form (History).

CHAPTER 2

Research objectives in this course

Students who master research skills for my course should be able to:

1.
2.
3.
4.
5.

?

Model transparency

For each research objective you want students to pursue, provide models to show students what the objective looks like in your field. Using the five examples listed above, models might include:

- Samples of research and thesis questions of appropriate scope and topic.
- Samples of hypotheses that explain purpose.
- Examples of data that are relevant to audiences.
- Sample paragraphs drawing on a variety of sources.
- Examples of viable historical research questions expressed effectively.

CHAPTER 2

Schedule brief reviews of student work

For each research objective you want students to pursue, schedule time for criterion-based conversations about student achievement in their writing:

- Where does the work establish that it's of an appropriate scope and topic?
- Where does the work include a hypothesis that clearly states the purpose of the work?
- Where does the work include relevant/irrelevant data specifically in terms of audience concerns?
- Where does the work include content that draws on a variety of sources?
- Where does the work express an effective, viable historical research question?

Give students tools for adapting based on what they learn during reviews

Personal editing checklists: instruct students to add genre/structure strategies to their checklists after each review, such as:

- Review source validity.
- Narrow your research question by [human impact, time period, location, or other criteria].
- Reflect on the purpose of data—what reader-centered need does it meet?
- Support claims from multiple sources—not only one.
- Refine historical research question by [course guidelines for viable research questions].

CHAPTER 2

Step 4: Introduce students to genre/structure objectives

Because genres and structures of disciplinary writing vary widely, orienting students to genre/structure objectives in your course helps to focus student attention on content, purpose, and organization best-suited to their discipline.

Getting started

Outline genre/structure objectives you have for students in your course. Arriving at five or more objectives helps students see a variety of ways to meet objectives and reveals the forms you value in your field.

Faculty definitions of genre/structure and their manner of describing related skills, knowledge, or outcomes vary widely, as the following examples of genre/structure abilities from faculty writing plans across the curriculum demonstrate:

- Write a research paper or report on a specific topic, question, problem, hypothesis, or model in the style of an article in a scientific journal (abstract, introduction, background, results, discussion, conclusion; proper citations) (Earth Sciences).
- Organize a paper so that it flows logically, perhaps using section headings (Psychology).
- Use appropriate structure…, opening with an introduction that discloses the scope and intent of the written work; dividing the whole into meaningful sections with headings that serve as guideposts for the reader; composing paragraphs that stand alone yet obviously relate to the preceding and subsequent paragraphs; presenting and discussing methods and/or evidence where they contribute most fruitfully to the reader's understanding; and closing with a summary (Geography, Environment, and Society).
- Recognize the expectations of genres, both as conventional modes of written expression and as elements of document design and organization, and possibly intentionally interrupt those expectations (Communication Studies).
- Organize material logically (Applied Economics).

CHAPTER 2

Genre/structure objectives in this course

Students who master genre/structure skills for my course should be able to:

1.
2.
3.
4.
5.

Model transparency

For each genre/structure objective you want students to pursue, provide models to show students what the objective looks like in your field. Using the five examples listed above, models might include:

- Samples of effective research papers or reports that feature appropriate topics, questions, problems, hypotheses in the appropriate style.
- Examples of logical flow and section headings appropriate to the genre
- Samples of appropriate structure as defined.
- Examples of relevant genres and interruptions of genre expectations.
- Examples of logical organization in your course.

CHAPTER 2

Schedule brief reviews of student work

For each genre/structure objective you want students to pursue, schedule time for criterion-based conversations about student achievement in their writing:

- Where does the work discuss topics, questions, problems, and hypotheses in the appropriate style?
- Where does the work achieve logical flow and appropriate section headings?
- Where does the work achieve appropriate structure?
- Where does the work meet and interrupt genre expectations?
- Where does the work achieve logical organization?

Give students tools for adapting based on what they learn during reviews

Personal editing checklists: instruct students to add research strategies to their checklists after each review, such as:

- Review assigned style guide and model topics, questions, problems, and hypotheses.
- To achieve logical flow, include [paragraph transitions, descriptive headings or other tactics discussed in class].
- Review content and organization requirements for the assigned genre.
- Review for opportunities to add interest by interrupting genre expectations.
- Review guidelines for logical structure.

CHAPTER 2

Step 5: Define synthesis objectives in your course

Instructors describe synthesis in a variety of ways from course to course, so providing explicit examples of synthesis for your course is likely to influence student writing in unique ways.

Getting started

Outline synthesis objectives you have for students in your course. Arriving at five or more objectives helps students see a variety of ways to meet objectives while providing insight into what synthesis should look like in your course.

Faculty definitions of synthesis and their manner of describing related skills, knowledge, or outcomes vary widely, as the following examples of synthesis abilities from faculty writing plans across the curriculum demonstrate:

- Deepen ideas to reach new levels of complexity (Theater Arts and Dance).
- Integrate visual, textual and oral explanations (Mechanical Engineering).
- Locate, understand, and apply relevant theories, concepts, and discipline-specific content to expand understanding of young people's everyday lives (Youth Studies).
- Highlight interaction of disparate ideas and link disparate ideas to create a new argument (Psychology).
- Apply scientific data to real-world situations and practical problems (Kinesiology).

CHAPTER 2

Synthesis objectives in this course

Students who master synthesis skills for my course should be able to:

1.
2.
3.
4.
5.

Model transparency

For each synthesis objective you want students to demonstrate, provide models to show students what the objective looks like in your field. Using the five examples listed above, models might include:

- Samples of deepened ideas, new levels of complexity from synthesis.
- Examples of effective visual, textual, and oral explanations according to discipline-specific practices.
- Samples of student writing or course readings that apply relevant theories.
- Examples of writing that creates a new argument from disparate ideas.
- Sample applications of data to real-world situations and practical problems.
- Schedule brief reviews of student work.

CHAPTER 2

For each genre/structure objective you want students to pursue, schedule time for criterion-based conversations about student achievement in their writing:

- Where does the work synthesize course content to achieve appropriate complexity?
- Where does the work integrate visual, textual, and oral explanations according to discipline-specific practice?
- Where does the work sufficiently apply relevant theories?
- Where does the work create a new argument from disparate ideas?
- Where does the work apply data to real-world situations and practical problems?

Give students tools for adapting based on what they learn during reviews

Personal editing checklists: instruct students to add research strategies to their checklists after each review, such as:

- In addition to including source information, discuss the value of source information.
- For each key idea, look for opportunities to integrate visual, textual, and oral explanations.
- Name the specific theory you are applying to ensure clarity.
- In addition to discussing others' arguments, add your own so it's clear what you think about the issue.
- Avoid hypothetical situations. Refer to real-world instances and practical problems instead of ones that might occur.

CHAPTER 2

Step 6: Introduce students to review/editing objectives

Providing explicit examples of review/editing objectives for your course helps make student efforts more productive.

Getting started

Outline review/editing objectives you have for students in your course. Arriving at five or more objectives helps students see a variety of ways to meet objectives while focusing their attention on high-priority tasks for improving their writing.

Faculty descriptions of review/editing requirements share common themes:

- Quote sources accurately; avoid plagiarism (Food Sciences and Nutrition).
- Cite sources in APS or other professional journal style (Physics).
- Use appropriate grammar, mechanics, spelling and style. Emphasize active construction (Journalism and Mass Communication).
- Engage in recursive writing processes involving self-assessment of drafts and revision (Anthropology).
- Students should understand the importance of revision and should be able to undertake it, not only by taking direction from instructor copy-edits and/or comments but also independently. Students should see writing as a multi-step process that involves brainstorming, outlining, drafting, and revisions (Geography, Environment, and Society).

CHAPTER 2

Review/editing objectives in this course

> Students who master review/editing skills for my course should be able to:
>
> 1.
> 2.
> 3.
> 4.
> 5.
>
> **?**

Model transparency

For each review/editing objective you want students to pursue, provide models to show students what the ability looks like in your field. Using the five examples listed above, models might include:

- Samples of valid/plagiarized source integration.
- Examples of appropriate style.
- Examples of common errors and how to avoid them.
- Peer review instructions; tools for self-assessment (editing checklist, for example).
- Samples of improved writing after review and revision; opportunities to use a multi-step process for brainstorming, outlining, drafting, and revision.

CHAPTER 2

Schedule brief reviews of student work

For each review/editing ability you want students to practice, schedule time for criterion-based conversations about student achievement in their writing:

- Where does the work integrate sources correctly/incorrectly?
- Where does the work adhere to/diverge from approved style?
- Where does the work include appropriate/inappropriate application of grammar, spelling, and mechanics?
- Where does the work demonstrate substantive revision based on self-assessment (using track changes, for example)?
- Where does the work show substantive revision based on feedback?

Give students tools for adapting based on what they learn during reviews

Personal editing checklists: instruct students to add review/editing strategies to their checklists after each review, such as:

- Check assignment guidelines for quoting and paraphrasing sources, using signal phrases, and including citations.
- Review styles for in-text citations and reference citations.
- Review run-ons and comma splices online. Check for noun/verb agreement.
- Do a search for "you" (second-person) and revise to achieve third-person style.
- After peer review, use "track changes" in MS Word, or the "Suggesting" mode in Google Docs so it's easy for me to see your additions, changes, and deletions.

CHAPTER 3

COLLABORATIVE WRITING ROLES AND TASKS FOR INTERDEPENDENT TEAMWORK

GUIDING QUESTIONS

- How do I define teammate roles?
- How do I devise teammate tasks?
- How do I identify individual contributions to collaboratively written content?
- How do I assign teammate roles?

CHAPTER 3

Interdependence in the classroom

In the workplace, hiring managers seek personnel who have a variety of expertise and experience so managers can create cross-functional teams. By *cross-functional*, we mean teams that think about the same problems from different functional points of view. For example, a web-development team might consist of a coder, a designer, a business analyst, and a usability specialist who create and test small parts of a website together. A business analyst thinks about sales goals and products to feature, a usability specialist thinks about users' interests and goals when visiting the site, the coder thinks about how to create functionality, and a designer thinks about page layout and visual design.

By working together on increments, or small parts, of the website and sharing ideas with each other from different professional perspectives, they learn about each other's ways of thinking about the website and quickly become productive based on what they learn together.

We can't always know who will enroll in our courses or what interests and experience students will bring. Instead of hiring on the basis of business objectives, as in the website example, we assign roles based on course learning objectives. Because students have not yet achieved enough mastery to work together cross-functionally, we emphasize interdependent learning instead. As with cross-functional teams of experts, interdependent teams of students think about the same problems from different points of view, but teammates use writing-to-learn strategies instead of product-development strategies.

CHAPTER 3

Roles for an interdependent writing process

A collaborative writing process is productive when teammates 1) have an expansive understanding of writing requirements from the beginning of the project and 2) a structure for pursuing requirements interdependently. That structure can be provided by teammate roles that support course learning objectives.

Research on roles in team-based learning describes the importance of assigned roles (Johnson, Johnson, & Smith, 2007), and the value of positive interdependence (Brewer & Klein, 2006) as keys to advancing writing and learning in teams. Assigned roles help teams work productively by focusing teammate attention on specific standards and tasks. Roles based on course learning objectives provide structure for interdependent learning.

Table 3.1. **Peer review roles named after learning objectives help immerse teams in relevant course content and writing objectives.**

Learning objectives	Peer review roles
Critical thinking	Critical thinking
Research	Research
Genre/structure	Genre/structure
Synthesis	Synthesis
Review/editing for professional publication	Review/editing for professional publication

When the names of interdependent roles for teammates correspond to the names of project objectives, instructors reinforce key goals and practices for students.

CHAPTER 3

Assigning writing tasks for teammates

As with objective-based roles, role-specific tasks help to align student behavior with key learning objectives. Tasks also help students see the complexity behind the most simple-sounding assignments and, as a result, budget their time more realistically. Writing a paragraph for a report, for example, may seem like a fairly simple activity. When we break the activity down by task, the complexity of the assignment is more evident.

Goal: Write a paragraph that compares the impact of repealing net neutrality on two startup companies.

Table 3.2. **Sample role-specific tasks for a writing assignment.**

Tasks	Instruction	Role-specific task
1	Find two sources about a startup that would be impacted by repeal of net neutrality (NN).	A research task that asks students to find two valid, relevant sources.
2	Describe similarities and differences between the two startups.	A critical thinking task.
3	Annotate sources.	A critical thinking task that involves multiple steps.
4	Write a claim that characterizes the impact of NN repeal.	A synthesis task requiring students to think critically about cause/effect, determine a basis for comparison between the startup companies, and formulate an original claim that accurately characterizes the impact.
5	Write an evaluative conclusion about the significance of the examples.	A synthesis task that asks students to reflect on the relationship of supporting examples to the claim they support.
6	Proofread your work.	A review/editing task that asks students to consider a variety of standards for professional publication in the discipline.

As the example above suggests, the complexity behind the most simple-sounding assignments can be significant. That complexity is one reason why students commonly underestimate how much time they need to complete writing projects.

CHAPTER 3

What roles ARE NOT

Before we outline roles for collaborative writing teams, we want to emphasize that the roles you create for teammates do not define the kinds of content teammates write for projects. The teammate in the research role is not solely responsible for doing the research for the team, for example. The teammate in the review/editing role is not solely responsible for proofreading, achieving technical accuracy, or performing other tasks commonly associated with review/editing.

> Roles correspond to objectives that all teammates should pursue while developing projects and drafting content.

What roles ARE

Roles represent learning objectives that all teammates should pursue while developing projects and drafting content. Teammate A is responsible for the quality of critical thinking, research, genre/structure, synthesis, review/editing in the work they contribute.

During peer review, however, teammates can also assist the whole team by assuming a single role and focusing their review comments on role-specific requirements. With one student focused on critical thinking objectives, and another on synthesis objectives, for example, role-specific peer review supports team productivity by helping to ensure depth and breadth of response during review.

CHAPTER 3

Teammate roles that correspond to the basic learning objectives create efficiencies for instructors when evaluating student work. The basic objectives of critical thinking, research, genre/structure, synthesis, and review/editing also support student learning during a common activity assigned across the curriculum: annotating sources. Using the same questions to guide annotating practices supports active reading of assigned texts while reinforcing key writing objectives:

Table 3.3. **Devising questions that students can use for annotating readings and drafts of team writing increases the frequency of student engagement with key objectives.**

	Critical thinking	Researching	Genre/structuring	Synthesis	Review/editing
Role-specific questions to ask while annotating sources and responding to teammate work.	Where does the work include a statement or reference to its purpose?	Where does the work include a research question and hypothesis?	Where does the work include correct content for the genre? Is content organized properly?	Where does the work include original conclusions drawn from source material?	Where do you see achievement (or lapses) in professional publishing practices?

Using the same heuristics for annotating sources as for drafting and peer review increases the amount of practice students gain working with course objectives, and while annotating, students see parallels between their achievement and the achievements of expert writers in their disciplines.

CHAPTER 3

Assigning course-specific tasks

The tasks you assign to each teammate writing role should support course learning objectives. Tasks should specify rhetorical moves and habits of mind that serve your course. The five basic objectives of critical thinking, research, genre/structure, synthesis, and review/editing provide a basic structure for tasks.

Critical thinking tasks
- Interpret an object of study.
- Compare multiple points of view to determine similarities and differences among them.
- Evaluate claims of validity in qualitative studies.

Research tasks
- Develop a research question of appropriate scope.
- Clearly and accurately visualize research results.
- Include a hypothesis to test in your analysis.

Genre/structure tasks
- Organize your work according to a valid model.
- Use figures and tables to clearly and accurately display research results.
- Use section headings to accurately orient readers to section content.

Synthesis tasks
- Provide concrete examples to support claims.
- Draw conclusions from source material.
- Use signal phrases to introduce source content.

Review/editing tasks
- Check your work for consistent use of verb tenses.
- Revise first draft to achieve consistent terminology.
- Revise so readers are not distracted by patterns of error.

CHAPTER 3

Redundancy on purpose

The point of assigning roles and tasks is to outline an explicit set of activities that align student writing efforts with course learning objectives. Especially during peer review, interdependent role and task assignments focus teammates' attention on specific project requirements, which students internalize over time and remember when developing their own content.

But the goal isn't to always make tasks exclusive to one role. Assigning the same task to more than one role helps differing opinions emerge for discussion. Assigning students in two different roles to discuss the key purpose of content they've developed together, for example, is likely to result in differing opinions about which purpose is primary and which are subordinate, helping teams to make decisions about content focus and team direction.

When assigned to student teams who work in a writing process for collaborative thinking, the roles and tasks you assign can give teammates the multiple perspectives they need to work productively—and interdependently—with each other.

To map writing projects, roles, and tasks to course learning objectives, we have outlined a process for reflecting on your course goals and ways that team writing can support students in achieving them. The process begins with your reflections on learning objectives, assigned readings, and assigned writing (Table 3.4).

- Column 1: List your course learning objectives.
- Column 2: List topics and genres of assigned readings (journal articles, textbooks, novels, cases, videos, for example).
- Column 3: List purpose and genres of assigned writing (analytical report, information graphic, multimedia content, persuasive essay, lab report, social media post, for example).

CHAPTER 3

Table 3.4. **Learning objectives, readings, and assigned writing.**

Course learning objectives	Assigned readings (topic and genre)	Assigned writing (purpose and genre)

How can writing tasks support course learning objectives?

With a list of learning objectives and genres to work from, you can outline writing tasks that support learning objectives. In the lists below, we have included examples of tasks that correspond with each objective. Modify the objectives and tasks to suit your preferences—they're provided only as a starting point for sorting and arranging types of writing tasks that support common learning objectives.

Critical thinking task examples
- Maintain appropriate tone: factual, professional (not colloquial).
- Include a statement about the work's purpose or focus.
- Maintain reader trust by citing valid sources as required.
- Define key terms as required.
- Interpret source material using paraphrases

CHAPTER 3

Research task examples
- Include signal phrases, paraphrases, and in-text citations as required.
- Include a list of references as required.
- Explain or illustrate human impact as required.
- Discuss cause and effect as required.
- Format and arrange references as required.

Genre/structure task examples
- Meet requirements for length, depth, and breadth.
- Include visuals as required.
  - » Include table and image numbers, captions, and citations as required.
- Include introductory information as required.
- Use descriptive headings and captions.
- Include all content sections.
- Meet content organization requirements.

Synthesis task examples
- Include topic sentence claims
- Include signal phrases, paraphrases, and citations as required
  - » Describe source validity.
  - » Interpret information from the source material accurately.
  - » Support topic sentence claims with paraphrased material.
  - » End paraphrases with source citations as required.
- Include comments about the value or significance of paragraph content as it relates to a thesis or other key idea.

Review/editing task examples
- Use terminology consistently.
- Make content free of distracting errors.
- Make the required number of comments or suggestions during peer review.
- Include all content sections.
- Cite all sources; prepare a reference list that meets requirements.

CHAPTER 3

Knowledge, skills, and writing tasks

1. Copy each objective supported by team writing into column 1 (Table 3.5).
2. Name the knowledge and skill you want students to demonstrate in their collaborative writing efforts.
3. Assign task categories best suited to each learning objective.

Table 3.5. **Devising objective-specific tasks helps instructors make writing expectations explicit by suggesting not only what to do but how.**

Course learning objectives	What knowledge/skill should students demonstrate in their collaborative writing efforts?	How should students demonstrate their knowledge?
Example learning objective: Demonstrate competence in quantitative data analysis.	*Ability to draw original conclusions from data.*	*Synthesis:* • *Make a claim about the significance of a data set.* • *Support your claim by referencing relevant source information.* • *Discuss the value of the conclusion(s) you've drawn.*

CHAPTER 3

Using roles and tasks during peer review

During a recent conversation with faculty about giving and receiving feedback on their own professional and scholarly writing, someone raised an interesting question. "If I frame my work in specific ways when asking peers for their responses, do I undermine truly authentic responses from readers?" Does asking for specific responses to specific questions limit the full value of the review process?

Some agreed that given the demands on our professional time, reading a peer's work with specific questions in mind helps bring focus and efficiency to the review process. They also acknowledged that at early stages of writing, asking a peer simply, "What do you think?" can be as valuable as more pointed questions about specific content in more fully developed work.

We have found that novice peer reviewers similarly benefit from having specific questions to ask—to make the time they spend responding more productive and to help build their capacities for delivering valuable peer review.

During the same conversation, we discussed a matter that weighs on novices and experts alike: "How do I make suggestions without hurting the author's feelings?" The question is important because vulnerability spikes among teammates during peer review whether they're the writers or the reviewers. Teammates want to be helpful, but they don't always know what helps and what might hurt.

That's why having a conversation about goals and techniques of peer review is so important: it's a way for teammates to gain empathy with each other while sharing their peer review experience as reviewers and as writers.

CHAPTER 3

Peer review and writers on the team

Assigning a discussion on the topic of peer review helps teammates get acquainted while uncovering preferences that can make teamwork more productive. Sample questions:

- How do you feel about commenting on teammates' writing?
- How do you feel about receiving comments from teammates about your writing?
- Which do you prefer: comments about what you've done well, so you know what to keep doing, or comments about specific project requirements and how to meet them?

Peer review and words on the page

Establishing peer review norms gives teams a jump-start on the peer review process. Some sample norms:

1. During review, start by identifying strengths. Where does the work meet expectations for focus, clarity, detail, or other high-level criteria?
2. Avoid commenting on grammatical or spelling errors. Highlighting them is usually sufficient, and there's no need to mark up every instance of the same problem or even every type of different problem.
3. Make internal comparisons. For examples:
   » "This paragraph doesn't seem as detailed as many of your paragraphs—paragraph 4 is especially thorough and interesting, so you could add more detail here to make it as good as paragraph 4."
   » "Your analysis on page 6 includes references two similar studies, which made your conclusion persuasive. This later analysis doesn't reference other studies, so it seems less effective."
   » "Would it work to use the same phrasing here as you used on page 2 so your wording is consistent?"

CHAPTER 3

Teammate roles during peer review

Teammate roles are useful throughout collaborative writing projects, but their value is perhaps easiest to imagine during the familiar activity of peer review. Roles increase the value of teammate feedback by providing each teammate with a narrow focus for reading and responding to drafts of teammates' work.

Although all teammates are required to meet the requirements of all roles (critical thinking, research, genre/structure, synthesis, review and editing), the person in the specified role provides support to the team by reviewing all increments and drafts according to course guidelines.

Ask students to label their peer review comments

To give students practice at applying their knowledge and skill, ask students to label their peer review comments according to the objectives you have set for their writing. The labels help teammates understand the purpose of each review comment, and they reveal to instructors the reviewers' understanding of objectives.

Critical thinking role for peer review

The teammate in the critical thinking role focuses on specific critical thinking tasks when peer reviewing all increments and drafts of the team's work (including their own).

These concepts have been applied to programs to test if they truly can lower crime rates. In professor Curry's lecture "Explanations for the Crime Drop and Social Benefits," she explains how programs that implement aspects of community outreach have been implemented successfully in Minnesota to build collective efficacy and help fight crime in a proactive, community engaging way.

The sources needed to determine the feasibility of whether or not a program that is utilized in a small town could be effective in a large city such as Houston are plentiful. An important aspect

K... Y...
3:38 PM Apr 14

CT: Introduce and give credibility to professor Curry, what does she teach?

Figure 6. **In the critical thinking role, a teammate suggests adding information about source credibility.**

CHAPTER 3

Research role for peer review

The teammate in the research role focuses on specific research tasks when peer reviewing all increments and drafts of the team's work (including their own).

Figure 7. **In the research role, a teammate reminds a collaborator to meet citation requirements.**

Genre/structure role for peer review

The teammate in the genre/structure role focuses on specific genre/structure tasks when peer reviewing all increments and drafts of the team's work (including their own).

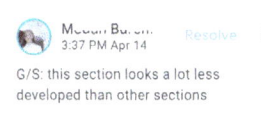

Figure 8. **In the genre/structure role, a teammate makes an internal comparison to promote additional content development.**

CHAPTER 3

Synthesis role for peer review

The teammate in the synthesis role focuses on specific paragraph/idea development tasks when peer reviewing all increments and drafts of the team's work (including their own).

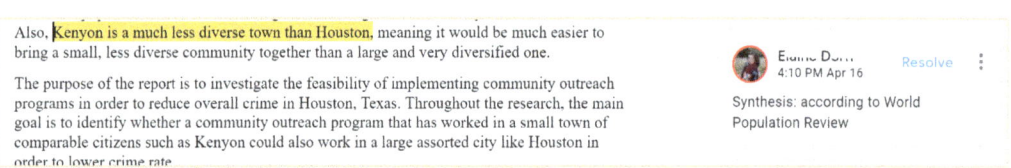

Figure 9. **A teammate in the synthesis role reminds a collaborator to indicate they have drawn their original conclusions by first consulting a valid source.**

Review and editing role for peer review

The teammate in the review and editing role focuses on specific review and editing tasks when peer reviewing all increments and drafts of the team's work (including their own).

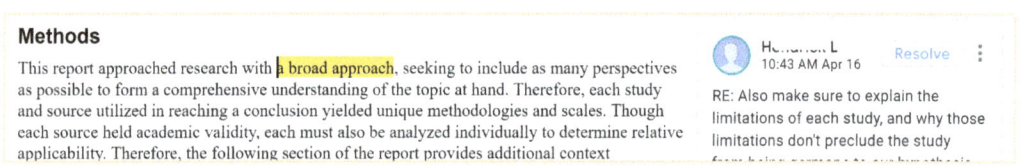

Figure 10. **In a note on a draft report, a teammate in the review/editing role suggests an addition.**

Sample critical thinking role for peer review

Asking students to pose role-specific questions helps focus attention and ensure that suggestions support key learning objectives. Modify the following questions to suit your course objectives for critical thinking.

Where does the work include a statement or heading in reference to its purpose?

Where does the work use a tone appropriate to audience/genre?

Where does the work establish and maintain trust at the beginning, in the main body, and at the end?

Where does the work define terms as required by the project?

Where does the work include a counter-argument that addresses a key issue?

Sample researching role for peer review

Asking students to pose role-specific questions helps focus attention and ensure that suggestions support key learning objectives. Modify the following questions to suit your course objectives for research.

Where does the work include a research question or hypothesis?

Where does the work discuss impact of a problem on specific people or groups accurately and in some detail?

Where does the work include signal phrases that introduce source material?

Where does the work discuss cause and effect as required?

Where does the work use scholarly or professional sources?

Sample genre/structuring role for peer review

Asking students to pose role-specific questions helps focus attention and ensure that suggestions support key learning objectives. Modify the following questions to suit your course objectives for genre/structure.

Where does the work include effective orientation content: descriptive headings and subheadings, topic sentences?

Where does the work include a complete, useful introduction appropriate to the genre?

Where does the work include a primary thesis or central argument?

Where does the work include all content sections appropriate to the genre, in appropriate order?

Where does the work include a counter-argument and refutation appropriate to the genre?

Sample synthesis role for peer review

Asking students to pose role-specific questions helps focus attention and ensure that suggestions support key learning objectives. Modify the following questions to suit your course objectives for synthesis.

Where do paragraphs include topic sentence claims as required, sufficient valid support for claims, and relevant logical conclusions?

Where does the work include signal phrases to introduce first use of each source?

Where does the work include evaluative paragraph conclusions?

Where does the work use paraphrases (not block quotations) and citations—and no lengthy quotations?

Is the counter-argument a complete, well-formed paragraph?

Sample review/editing role for peer review

Asking students to pose role-specific questions helps focus attention and ensure that suggestions support key learning objectives. Modify the following questions to suit your course objectives for review/editing (professional publication standards).

Where do you see errors in grammar or punctuation that you or teammates should revise?

Where does the work use appropriate paragraph styles and apply them accurately to all content?

Have all teammates reviewed the draft and made suggestions for improvement?

Have all teammates proofread their content so it is free of distracting errors?

Have authors revised according to their personal editing checklists?

CHAPTER 3

Options for assigning teammate roles

Instructors take a variety of approaches to assigning teammate roles, each of which has pros and cons:

Table 3.6. **Pros and cons of various teammate role assignment approaches.**

	Pros	Cons
Let teams decide	Teams have more agency; Students can select based on interests, strengths.	Teams may choose expediency over careful considerations; Individuals might not have a chance to develop a range of skills.
Instructor assigns roles based on data	Saves teams time; More instructor control.	May require more time for instructors to analyze student levels of interest and experience.
Rotate roles	Gives individuals a full range of experience.	Increased risks (but learning opportunities, too) when inexperienced teammates have roles for which they have low interest or little experience.
Instructor assigns roles randomly	Saves teams time; Saves instructor time.	Increased risks (but maybe learning opportunities, too) when inexperienced teammates have roles for which they have low interest or little experience.

Although assigning roles based on data is more time-consuming for instructors than other methods, we find that the time is well-spent for what instructors learn about students and how much more effective the effort is in devising well-balanced teams.

CHAPTER 3

Roles based on data

Instructors and student teams do have some data to work with when forming teams and assigning roles. One way to balance teams is to first complete the following Interest/Confidence Inventory.

After students are familiar with a project, ask them to consider their levels of interest and confidence in contributing to the project by including a two-number set for each learning objective/role.

For example, under critical thinking, each teammate will have a number set:

- **6/2:** This set means relatively high interest and relatively low confidence in the role.
- **3/7:** This set means some interest and high confidence in the role.

Giving students a chance to share their interest and confidence levels helps teammates learning about each others' objectives for the course.

Having low confidence does not mean a student shouldn't take a role; having high interest but low confidence means a student wants to build their confidence in that area by gaining experience with the role and the assigned tasks.

Similarly, knowing which teammates have high confidence and low interest is helpful. Perhaps students have a lot of experience with review and editing and have high confidence in their abilities; that's good for the whole team to know. But if a student has done so much review and editing that they want to work on a different skill, they should give the Interest rating for review/editing a low number. All teammates need to know about teammate confidence and interest in order to take advantage of strengths and manage risk during projects.

CHAPTER 3

Example of interest/confidence inventory

Table 3.7 shows a sample documentation of students' Interest/Confidence ratings. Teammates may add their own name and rating for each basic role.

Table 3.7. **Sample interest/confidence inventory form.**

Teammate Interest (I) and Confidence (C) Low 1 2 3 4 5 6 7 High					
Teammate name	Critical thinking	Research	Genre/structure	Synthesizing ideas	Review/editing
Sample Bob	4/4	5/3	2/2	2/3	3/3
Sample Jane	3/4	3/4	5/3	2/5	3/6
name	I/C	I/C	I/C	I/C	I/C
name	I/C	I/C	I/C	I/C	I/C
name	I/C	I/C	I/C	I/C	I/C
name	I/C	I/C	I/C	I/C	I/C

Teamwork experience essays

Knowing students' past experience with team writing is useful in avoiding team rosters that include only students who have had mostly negative or only those who have had mostly positive team writing experiences in the past. A short essay assignment at the beginning of the course provides a useful introduction to your students. A modified essay assignment near the end of the course, asking whether students' experience has been mostly positive or negative, provides direction for modifying learning experiences and materials.

Essay prompt early in the course
Tell a story in response to the following prompt: I have had mostly positive/negative [choose one] experiences in team writing projects in the past (150 words, minimum).

CHAPTER 3

If you have no past team writing experience, tell a story about any college writing experience and what made it positive or negative.

Responses provide several kinds of valuable information:
1. Student attitudes toward collaborative writing
2. What students perceive to be positive and negative about collaborative writing
3. An introduction to students' writing experience
4. An introduction to students' writing styles
5. Who in the course has had no collaborative writing experience

Essay prompt late in the course
Tell a story (150 words, minimum) in response to the following prompt: I have had mostly positive/negative [choose one] experiences in team writing projects this semester.

Creating a role/task board

Students report that having this master board helps them see how their work is related to the work of teammates. It also provides a global view of project objectives. The role/task board should outline the scope of your project and give teammates a guide to all project objectives.

The example in Table 3.8 features the basic objectives for collaborative writing and a set of tasks that support each objective. As a whole, the role/task board comprises a rubric for individual performance. By role, the board also details specific questions to ask during formative and draft review of collaboratively written materials.

CHAPTER 3

Table 3.8. **Sample role/task board for teams.**

Critical thinking role	Researching role	Genre/ structuring role	Synthesis role	Review/editing role
Where does the work include a statement or heading in reference to its purpose?	Where does the work include a research question or hypothesis?	Where does the work include effective orientation content: descriptive headings and subheadings, topic sentences?	Where do paragraphs include topic sentence claims as required, sufficient valid support for claims, and relevant logical conclusions?	Where do you see errors in grammar or punctuation that you or teammates should revise?
Where does the work use an appropriate tone?	Where does the work discuss the impact of a problem on specific people or groups accurately and in some detail?	Where does the work include a complete, useful introduction appropriate to the genre?	Where does the work include signal phrases to introduce first use of each source?	Where does the work use appropriate paragraph styles & apply them accurately to all content?
Where does the work establish & maintain trust at the beginning, in the main body, and at the end?	Where does the work include signal phrases that introduce source material?	Where does the work include a primary thesis or central argument?	Where does the work include evaluative paragraph conclusions?	Have all teammates reviewed the draft & made suggestions for improvement?
Where does the work define terms as required by the project?	Where does the work discuss cause & effect as required?	Where does the work include all content sections appropriate to the genre, in appropriate order?	Where does the work use paraphrases (no block quotes) & citations--and no lengthy quotations?	Have all teammates proofread their content so it is free of distracting errors?
Where does the work include a counter-argument that addresses a key issue?	Where does the work use scholarly or professional sources?	Where does the work include a counter-argument & refutation appropriate to the genre?	Is the counter-argument a complete, well-formed paragraph?	Have authors revised according to their personal editing checklists?

CHAPTER 4

AN INTERDEPENDENT LEARNING ENVIRONMENT FOR COLLABORATIVE WRITING

GUIDING QUESTIONS

- What is an interdependent writing environment for teams?
- How can I support an interdependent writing environment for teams?
- How should teams structure discussions to ensure interdependent teamwork?
- How can classroom activities support the values of transparency, review, and adaptation?
- Which norms for teamwork, cooperation, and collaboration support interdependence?
- How can a team charter help establish an interdependent writing environment for teams?

CHAPTER 4

Collaborative writing is so different from individual writing that, in addition to the writing process (Chapter 5), the environment in which collaborative writing takes place should be redesigned, too. By environment we mean more than how the furniture is arranged, although enabling teammates to sit together is always a good idea.

By learning environment for writing teams, we mean a set of values that build an atmosphere of trust—in the classroom and in small groups. An atmosphere of trust is important because students report a variety of fears about writing—whether they're writing individually or in teams—that add up to an overarching feeling of vulnerability. All students feel fear at some point and writing in teams has a way of heightening individuals' feelings of vulnerability. The fear of sounding stupid, being wrong, not measuring up, not carrying their own weight. Fear of not knowing where to start, how to end, what to say. In *The Courage to Write*, author Ralph Keyes (1995) observes that the prevailing feeling that consumes even the most revered writers—Margaret Atwood, Gabriel Garcia Marquez, Cynthia Ozick, and E.B. White among them—is fear. Add the pressures of coursework, relative inexperience, and collaborative writing to the mix, and fears among students can spike.

Characteristics of an interdependent learning environment:

- Students are invited, instructed, and supported in interdependent writing
- Projects are complex enough to promote interdependence
- Teammates have roles and assigned tasks
- Students are rewarded for making thinking visible
- Students are rewarded for reviewing teammates' work
- Students are rewarded for adapting to learning
- Instructor assesses interdependent learning
- Instructor emphasizes formative assessment
- Instructor assigns class time for team discussions and team writing

CHAPTER 4

Three core values for sustaining a collaborative learning environment

An environment that sustains productive collaborative learning promotes values of transparency, review, and adaptation inside and outside of class:

- **Transparency:** Enabling students to make thinking—and learning—visible; making instructor thinking and learning visible.
- **Review:** Accommodating frequent discussions about content that teams and teammates develop.
- **Adaptation:** Welcoming change based on 1) what students learn about each other and their project—and 2) what instructors learn about students.

Transparency

The value of transparency, or making thinking and learning visible, contributes to a productive environment by reassuring students that they're not "in it alone," that they understand more—or less—than they think they do. Students report that their confidence rises when they discover that they're not the only ones who aren't sure what to do or don't fully grasp course content. Working together on shared documents reveals to some that their writing "weaknesses" aren't as weak as they thought. They learn, in some cases, that abilities they have perhaps discounted or taken for granted in the past have high value among teammates.

Instructors model the value of transparency by making their thinking visible too—in the form of explicit learning objectives, of models that illustrate what they mean by, for example, "clear writing," "creativity," "synthesis," or "original research." Instructors who share what they have learned in past courses, and as the current course plays out, demonstrate that learning never stops and that expertise evolves.

CHAPTER 4

We've found that students are willing to make their thinking visible when we pose specific questions about matters that affect their grades: for example, periodically asking teammates to describe obstacles they face while trying to perform tasks on behalf of the team. Some students respond by naming obstacles to their understanding of course content or assignments. Frequently, students report obstacles such as "Hockey game," "parents visiting," "Halloween," "birthday party," and a host of other events that compete for their time. Many also cite "working 20 hours," "studying for exams in other courses," and "finishing homework for other courses" as persistent obstacles to productivity. An environment that values transparency is likely to reveal to instructors and teammates the reality that everyone works according to their priorities.

While we knew that students had other courses and that many were working at least part-time—if not more—we never felt as clearly how time pressures constantly weigh on students' minds as when we asked them to be honest about what they could and could not commit to finishing by their due dates. Our new understanding hasn't changed the workloads we assign—we have our own academic commitments to meet—but the information helps teammates, and us as instructors, achieve deeper empathy with the students in our courses.

Empathy is important to making collaborative writing projects successful because it mitigates finger-pointing—a behavior that seriously undermines trust. Also in play, and among the most difficult issues to address, include realities that have a significant impact on student behavior: food (in)security, safety at home and on campus; (dis)ability, health (physical and mental), whiteness, citizenship status, racism, and transphobia; and interpersonal factors including how students see themselves and see and are seen by classmates and instructors. Therefore, classrooms and teammates must balance transparency while honoring boundaries, or what students and instructors feel safe to share. A productive environment therefore may invite participants to safely say, "I am facing other significant obstacles right now, but I don't want to share them."

CHAPTER 4

Transparency should reveal teammate preferences that affect project-specific small group dynamics. Take the example of preferences about completing tasks. Many students prefer to get work off their plates as soon as possible. They prefer to do their work well ahead of deadlines. Other students are more productive when they're closer to their deadlines. When off-the-plate students perceive last-minute students as irresponsible, when last-minute students feel dogged by off-the-platers, team dynamics suffer. Transparency about priorities and preferences helps reduce anxiety. It does not alleviate all anxiety, but it does improve empathy and gives rise to conversations about communicating early and often about progress. An environment that supports transparency therefore has not only to invite honesty but be adaptive to change.

Sustaining transparency inside and outside of class

Using Google Docs, Sheets, and Slides—or any platform that enables students to collaborate on shared files and comment on teammate work synchronously or asynchronously—contributes significantly to transparency. Your learning management system (LMS) is likely to have collaboration tools, and commercial platforms such as Dropbox or Microsoft Office 365 have developed apps to meet the demand for collaborative writing tools. Using online tools may present accessibility issues for some students. Your campus's disability resource center can provide guidelines for ensuring that collaboration platforms are accessible to all team members, with suggestions for chunking content, using headings, and formatting content with bullets or numbered lists, among other simple tactics, that can make your students' online experience more productive.

CHAPTER 4

Review

Brief but frequent review supports writing teams by providing reassurance or redirection. Unlike environments in which review of written work occurs only after students have written complete drafts, a team writing environment should include frequent presentations of written increments for review. Frequent formative feedback—versus rare summative feedback—provides valuable direction before teammates invest large amounts of time following potentially unproductive paths.

In a classroom environment, the small parts—or increments—can be titles, phrases, headings, sentences, snippets of a video, or a rough website wireframe. They don't have to be long because review questions target specific learning objectives and ask how the increments represent progress in achieving them. Traditional writing process models for individuals typically wait until students have invested large amounts of time producing whole drafts of a work before peer or instructor review. Comprehensive review can be valuable, too, but if it's the sole mode of peer or instructor response and if it comes only after long periods of content development, the response can be too much too late.

Frequent review of increments takes less time for response from instructors and provides students with more timely direction. When using collaborative writing, instructors can address comments to all teammates at once instead of repeating them for individual students. Frequent review also helps students improve the value of their own peer review comments, over time, through practice.

CHAPTER 4

Adaptation

The value of adaptation in a collaborative writing environment refers to a prevailing expectation that learning should lead to changes in thinking and behavior. During projects students commonly adapt their writing because of what they learn about readers, teammates, topics, and genre; they change their behaviors based on what they learn about the value of the content they've developed, of their communication with teammates, of the research they've conducted. Teams apply the adaptation principle in several ways:

1. Teams adapt written work based on what they learn about writing during frequent review.
2. Teams adapt processes based on what they learn about their productivity during team retrospective meetings (Chapter 5) in which they discuss what's working, what isn't working, and how they will change their practices during the next phase of their work together.
3. Instructors adapt learning materials and classroom practices based on what they learn about student interpretations of project objectives during increment reviews.

CHAPTER 4

What does the collaborative writing environment look like in practice?

Activities that contribute to a safe collaborative writing environment help teammates see and discuss the instructor's and each other's understanding of course learning objectives.

Activities for practicing transparency

- For each requirement in your collaborative writing project, provide a model that shows how it aligns with learning objectives.
- In your current course, identify specific student ideas, traits of student work, or traits of professional models and explain how they align with specific learning objectives.
- Show examples of student achievement from past courses and how they align with learning objectives.
- Assign team update memos where teammates post tasks they commit to performing, how much time they plan to dedicate to the tasks, and by when they plan to complete them.
- Encourage honesty about when teammates will complete tasks. Assign discussions about teammate expectations for communication.
- Assign discussions in which teammates share their calendars and preferred work styles (do individuals do work as soon as it's assigned or do they wait until the last minute?) How do individuals' preferred work styles affect others on the team?

CHAPTER 4

Activities for collaborating inside and outside of class

- Include time for team meetings inside and outside of class on the project calendar.
- Hold collaborative writing sessions during class.
- Assign low-stakes practice sessions on a collaborative writing platform.

Activities for practicing frequent review

- Show examples of past project work, and ask teams to discuss how it could be improved to meet project objectives.
- Assign brief but frequent discussions about increments created by teammates (increment review) and ask students to discuss how the increments meet project objectives.
- Assign brief but frequent annotations of assigned readings, teammate drafts, or the source materials they intend to use.
- Assign brief team retrospective meetings for teammates to discuss what's working, what's not working, and how they should improve their cooperation and collaboration.

CHAPTER 4

Activities for practicing adaptation

- Assign tasks whose results tell you how students are interpreting your assignments and expectations.
- Give short (two-minute) writing assignments: "Put requirement X into your own words (paraphrase it). Compare your paraphrases with teammates." Affirm or redirect teams based on what you learn from their interpretations.
- Near the end of some class sessions, ask teams to discuss their next high-priority tasks. Affirm or redirect teams based on what you learn.
- Periodically assign teams to discuss their productivity: what's working, what isn't working, how will they change their practices in order to improve productivity?
- After reviewing increments, assign teams to list high-priority tasks for putting to work what they have learned.
- Assign teams to present increments to each other, discuss how they align with learning objectives, and make suggestions for adapting increments to make them more valuable to the team's project.

CHAPTER 4

The team learning environment

The team learning environment is subject to a variety of influences that can promote or discourage effective collaboration. Two instructor practices can get teams off to a good start: create equitable teams and assign a team charter activity.

Creating equitable teams

To create equitable teams, instructors might consider a variety of factors:

- The diversity of students' academic interests, experience, and skills.
- Diversity of writing experience.
- Range of writing skills.
- Personal and cultural variables related to issues of equity:
    » Implicit bias—attitudes, stereotypes, and unintentional actions—whether they are positive or negative—may manifest among teammates because members perceive others as being members of a group. For example, Asian, Black, Latinx, Native American, or White;
    » Historically underrepresented groups and new immigrant populations;
    » People with both apparent and non-apparent disabilities;
    » Gender identity and expression: nonbinary people, cis- and trans- women and men;
    » People of various gender and sexual identities and expressions; and
    » First-generation students from economically disadvantaged backgrounds.

CHAPTER 4

Instructors take a variety of approaches to assigning individuals to teams, each of which has pros and cons.

Table 4.1. **Pros and cons of approaches to teammate role assignment.**

	Pros	Cons
Let teams self-select	Teams perceive more agency Students might feel more confidence	Friends use familiar practices instead of effective practices Lack of diversity
Instructor assigns teams based on data	Saves teams time More instructor control	May require more time for instructors to analyze student levels of interest and experience.
Change teams for each project	Students work with the highest number of different students	Teams don't get a chance to learn about each other and get used to ways of working
Instructor assigns teams randomly	Saves teams time Saves instructor time	Likely to result in unequal teams: some very strong; some very inexperienced Likely to result in isolation for some students

Given the complexity and the importance of equity, we suggest that instructors assign students to teams. While achieving equity in teams is a persistent challenge, early assignments and activities can provide data on which to base your decisions:

1. Short essays on past team-writing experiences (was it mostly positive or mostly negative?) so you can include students who've had positive experiences on each team.
2. Attitude surveys about course content or team writing, so you can achieve a balance of attitudes.

CHAPTER 4

3. In-class writing samples for assessing writing skills so you can create teams balanced by a variety of skills and experience.
4. Interest/confidence survey (see Chapter 3), so you can balance teams by student interests and levels of confidence.

All methods for creating teams have flaws, and time constraints prevent us all from performing enough research on individual students to achieve a truly equitable mix of knowledge and skills. Nevertheless, we suggest that instructors create teams because doing so comes closest to achieving advantages most worth pursuing on behalf of collaborative writing teams:

Presence of
- Diverse interests
- Diverse academic experience
- Diverse writing experience
- Diverse identities (by gender identity and expression, country of origin, major, academic year, for example)

Absence of
- Friend cliques
- Academic major cliques
- Extracurricular activity cliques
- Identity-based isolation (by gender identity and expression, country of origin, major, academic year, for example)

CHAPTER 4

Team charter activity

While few would argue against the value of accountability, few are skilled in holding others accountable while also maintaining teammate trust. In the workplace, teammates have extrinsic motivations for earning strong performance reviews and keeping their jobs. Students on collaborative writing teams have competing priorities that can undermine strong performance, such as other coursework, family commitments, and jobs, to name a few. The Team Charter Activity is designed to bring those issues to the surface so teammates have realistic expectations of each other.

Spending time on a team charter at the beginning of the first collaborative writing project sets the tone for one of the most critical elements of a team's writing environment: the demeanor and practices of teammates. To focus team attention on goals for participation, cooperation, and collaboration, the team charter discussion raises important questions about how teammates can work together productively while surfacing individual assumptions and preferences. "Discussion topics for the team charter" outlines basic expectations and, in brackets, associated questions for team discussion.

Discussion topics for the team charter

Actively participates (practices teamwork)

Attends class meetings.
Discuss advantages of attending class meetings; discuss problems that arise when someone misses class meetings.

Contributes to team discussions.
How do individuals on your team prefer to contribute to team discussion?

Shares leadership.
How do all teammates feel about taking a leadership role? What do teammates consider their leadership strengths?

Completes a fair share of the work.
Discuss examples of fair and unfair amounts of work.

Complies with others' requests (is cooperative)

Responds to teammate messaging within the time frame agreed upon by the team.
Determine a time frame that everyone agrees on.

Completes tasks on time.
What problems arise when someone completes tasks later than they said they would? Who will send reminders about late/missing work? How many reminders will you send?

Notifies teammates before absences or missed deadlines.
Why is notifying teammates about absences or missed deadlines ahead of time important? Who will keep track when teammates don't notify the team?

Behaves respectfully toward teammates in meetings.
What are some examples of respectful and disrespectful behaviors?

Accepts or respectfully negotiates when others disagree with their ideas during discussions.
Discuss examples of respectful negotiation during disagreements.

Expresses support for teammates' opinions or ideas during discussions.
What kinds of support do teammates appreciate?

Discussion topics, cont.

Works toward shared goals (collaborates)

> **Proposes (but not forces) ideas, suggestions, courses of action.**
> What are some examples of proposing ideas too forcefully?
>
> **Asks teammates for their opinion.**
> When do teammates feel most comfortable sharing their opinions?
>
> **Builds on teammate ideas.**
> Discuss examples of ways you have built on others' ideas.
>
> **Offers to help teammates.**
> What kinds of help do teammates appreciate?
>
> **Invites views or opinions from team members who are not actively participating in the discussion.**
> How do teammates feel about inviting others to participate? What are some effective ways of inviting participation?

Options for meeting outside of class

> What are some of our most realistic options for meeting outside of class? When could you meet? Face-to-face or online?
>
> How many of you use Google video calls, Skype, or other conferencing tools?
>
> How should we share calendars?
>
> What is the best way to communicate with teammates (e.g. email, text, phone call, app)?

CHAPTER 4

Upon completing the team charter discussion, teammates should co-author their charter using an outline that corresponds to the questions you present to teams.

Team charter

All teammates agree to abide by the following team charter:

Participation

Cooperation

Collaboration

Options for meeting outside of class

CHAPTER 4

Team charters can be rich with insights about student priorities, preferences, and attitudes—insights that are valuable to teammates and instructor alike, as suggested by these excerpts:

> "Our main mode of communication will be in class, over groupme, and Google Hangouts whenever possible. Everyone's opinions are valued and considered during discussions. Some teammates like communicating during discussion. Some teammates like to mull over an idea at home before talking about it"

> "One example of a respectful negotiation was last semester when I had a group member who did not respond to messaging. When [they] did, [they] apologized and gave an explanation why. We gave [the teammate] the rundown and what [they] had to do and we were good to go. However, I was once in a group where one person did all the work and scrutinized anyone that tried to do anything."

> "Our group is split between those who [prefer to] finish work early, and those who prefer to work closer to the deadline. We will split the work so that members of the group who prefer to work earlier can do so. We will also attempt to finish work the night before when dealing with an 11:15am deadline, and by 6:00pm the same day with an 11:59pm deadline."

> "Our most realistic options for meeting outside of class are Wednesdays, from 6:00pm to 6:30pm. We can meet online using the program 'Zoom.us.' Additional in-person meetings will happen in the Cube (Coffman Memorial Union). We have all dabbled in other modes of communication such as Google video and Skype; however, we feel that Zoom is our best option to meet online. We plan to communicate by text and share if we cannot meet deadlines through messages. We have a group message and have agreed to check our messages at least once every 24 hours."

CHAPTER 5

A WRITING PROCESS FOR INTERDEPENDENT COLLABORATION

GUIDING QUESTIONS

- How do I provide meaningful feedback to teams efficiently?
- How can I measure team and teammate productivity?
- How should I provide feedback on collaboratively written materials?
- How should teams conduct peer reviews?
- How should I design a rubric that supports course learning objectives?
- How should teammates annotate sources?

CHAPTER 5

Students appreciate writing and learning with each other. Students report feelings of pride in the contributions they make. They gain confidence in their writing and problem-solving ability while working together toward shared goals, and their observations about what makes collaborative writing a positive experience illustrate an awareness of the many ways their learning has depended on contributions from teammates:

- Consulting with each other frequently about individual progress and priorities.
- Setting deadlines for the team and committing to tasks, both verbally and electronically.
- Seeing your strengths and weaknesses; you can learn a lot from your partners.
- My writing is so concise so I was able to shorten my teammates' writing so our papers were more to the point and professional.
- Sharing pride in our work.
- Helping me not only identify and hone my strengths as a writer but also discovering ways to compensate for my weaknesses.
- Teammate comments helped me improve my writing.
- Working as a team on a report raised ideas I hadn't thought of
- I learned a lot about myself.
- Meetings taught me how to work well in a team.
- You have others that you can ask that might be having a similar problem.

CHAPTER 5

- I feel as though I could have been a bigger contributor and that is something I wish to work on in the future.
- For my team members who struggle with writing, I used some of my editing techniques to help explain to them where clarity was lost/why grammar was incorrect.
- Changed my writing style and strengthened my skills.
- Improved my confidence.
- I've been putting my best work forward.
- I found myself keeping better track of time to keep up with my team members.
- When I thought of suggestions to give teammates, I sometimes ended up applying my suggestion to my own work.
- Gave me the confidence I needed to work well in a group writing.
- Changed perspective of team writing from negative to positive.
- Prepared me for future team project.

But not all writing processes support productive, positive collaboration. Serial writing process models can be ineffective for teams if feedback (peer review and instructor response) 1) occurs only late in the drafting stage and 2) serves mainly the purpose of helping writers polish their work before submitting it for evaluation.

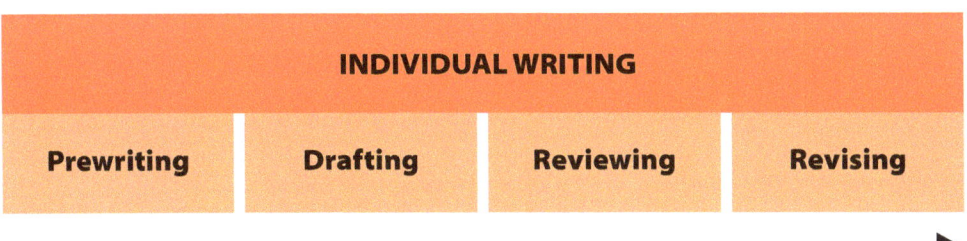

Figure 11. **The serial writing process.**

CHAPTER 5

A serial writing process model is useful for students working alone because it helps individuals manage the complexity of writing in a divide/conquer approach that promotes reflection about goals (prewriting), content generation (drafting), reader response (review), and refinement (revision).

The collaborative writing process we outline in this chapter also divides to conquer, but it departs significantly from serial process models in two fundamental ways: 1) by emphasizing positive interdependence among teammates, and 2) by including a framework for interdependent problem solving.

Positive interdependence among teammates

Missing from serial writing process models for individuals, positive interdependence is the foundation of a writing process for teams. As David W. Johnson, Roger T. Johnson, and Karl Smith (2007) explain, "Positive interdependence exists when individuals perceive that they can reach their goals if and only if the other individuals with whom they are cooperatively linked also reach their goals and, therefore, promote each other's efforts to achieve the goals" (p. 23). Positive interdependence among student teammates exists when individuals perceive the true complexity of writing: how critical thinking, researching, genre/structuring, synthesizing, and review/editing operate interdependently from the very beginning and for the duration of projects. That is, to manage complexity in writing teams, a collaborative writing process requires teams to reflect on project complexity during prewriting, drafting, review, and revision.

CHAPTER 5

Figure 12 illustrates basic differences between the serial process for independent writing, above, and a parallel process for interdependent collaborative writing. Two features of the model below are worth highlighting: 1) its emphasis on increments of content instead of drafts of content, and 2) its design for teammates working together in parallel.

Teammates consider project requirements during prewriting, content development, peer review, and revision.

TEAM WRITING			
Prewriting	**Drafting**	**Reviewing**	**Revising**
Empathizing	Empathizing	Empathizing	Empathizing
Defining	Defining	Defining	Defining
Prototyping	Prototyping	Prototyping	Prototyping
Reviewing	Reviewing	Reviewing	Reviewing
Reflecting as a team	Reflecting as a team	Reflecting as a team	Reflecting as a team

Figure 12. **A parallel process for interdependent collaborative writing.**

CHAPTER 5

Increments of content

An increment is a small segment of content that teams consider finished—a title, a subject heading, a few sentences, an image. A writing process for collaborative writing teams includes frequent review of increments instead of infrequent review of complete drafts so teammates can test their assumptions about project goals against those of teammates and instructor.

As with completed drafts in a serial process, an increment is the result of prewriting and drafting. Because the increment is short, so is the time required for review and feedback. When the writing process includes structured activities for subjecting increments to frequent review, teams receive valuable direction early and often.

Teammates working together in parallel

To support authentic interdependence, a collaborative writing process must emphasize the interdependence of the five key project requirements—critical thinking, research, genre/structure, synthesis, and review/editing—throughout the project. Interdependence is a powerful concept in collaborative writing because it is an attribute of effective teams and of effective writing. In writing, the effectiveness of conclusions depends on the effectiveness of research. Research is dependent on critical thinking. Changes in genre require changes in research. Expert writers are aware of ways that genres guide content and organization, but students' understanding of unfamiliar genres competes with their understanding of conventions with which they are most familiar. Achieving consensus about genres and other project requirements is therefore a central pursuit of writing teams.

CHAPTER 5

The example of synthesis is especially complex. Instructor expectations for synthesis—and the vocabulary they use to express those expectations—vary significantly by course. For example, instructors in different courses ask students to achieve synthesis by:

1. **Situating** their writing within the broader questions and themes of the discipline (anthropology).
2. **Finding their own voices** and conveying individual perspectives and points of view in a logical and convincing manner (applied economics).
3. **Drawing evidence-based conclusions** and discussing their implications (political science).
4. **Applying knowledge** of physics, mathematics, and engineering in their writing (mechanical engineering).

What students should do to meet expectations for synthesis is neither universal nor self-evident, so frequent conversations about synthesis requirements help students work together to meet synthesis requirements. A writing process that structures conversations about expectations for synthesis and other requirements gives students a chance to pursue consensus and deepen their understanding of key course concepts.

CHAPTER 5

During all phases of projects—from prewriting through final review—teammates can explore the interdependence of the five requirements of critical thinking, research, genre/structure, synthesis, and review/editing through structured activities.

1. During **team meetings** by interpreting requirements differently from each other and comparing teammate understanding of requirements and how to meet them:
    - Early in the project while defining teammates roles and tasks for critical thinking, research, genre/structure, synthesis, and review/editing.
    - Throughout projects during team update meetings.
    - Periodically during team retrospective meetings.
2. During **increment reviews** by discussing how increments meet objectives for:
    - Critical thinking
    - Research
    - Genre/structure
    - Synthesis
    - Review/editing
3. During **peer reviews** by offering reminders about specific requirements—for example, the need to:
    - Interpret course content accurately, to interpret source materials thoroughly and purposefully (Critical thinking).
    - Fully addressing research questions; citing sources accurately (Research).
    - Include relevant content, organized appropriately according to genre guidelines (Genre/structure).
    - Sufficiently integrate source material; providing original insights (Synthesis).
    - Thoroughly review and revise work according to discipline-specific guidelines for professional publication (Review/editing).

CHAPTER 5

A process for interdependent problem solving

So far, we have outlined a process for teammates working together interdependently in ways that model the interdependence of basic writing activities. Because interdependence places unique demands on teammates, a process for collaborative writing also requires a framework for teams to use while addressing problems they are charged with writing about and for addressing problems that emerge when pursuing learning objectives through collaboration and cooperation.

We use the familiar phrase *writing process* with some reservations. On the one hand, writing and process accurately represent the reality that we all proceed with one activity at a time even while engaged in the complex work of writing. As a heuristic for students, *process* is a useful heuristic for sorting writing into manageable types of tasks, and *writing* is a useful shorthand for naming the product of that process. But writing also represents activities other than putting words on the page: seeking understanding, reflecting on diverse points of view, and testing ideas are as essential to writing as typing, doodling, or writing longhand. *Process* is equally reductive in failing to account for the editing we do during prewriting, the review we conduct while drafting, and the problem-solving we engage in every step of the way. The positive interdependence model, above, is a step toward a less reductive heuristic.

A second step is to outline an interdependent problem-solving framework for collaborative writing teams. In what follows, we outline a framework that draws from design thinking, a human-centered process featuring empathy, definition, prototyping, increment review, and team retrospective for exploring solutions to complex problems.

CHAPTER 5

 Empathizing

We commonly ask students—and professionals, for that matter—to empathize with their audiences so they come to understand audience needs, interests, and experience levels well enough to develop relevant information. Empathizing with audiences—understanding how they feel about problems and solutions—is a basic step in writing whether authors are working alone or in teams. Therefore, empathizing is a starting point of prewriting.

For writing teams to be productive, they must not only understand their audiences, but they must similarly explore teammates' needs and experience levels to avoid making false assumptions about each other that can undermine productive collaboration.

Interdependence can be demanding, so teammates need information and support from each other in order to work independently. Teammates have differing skills and interests; they all manage competing priorities. They have differing writing experience, teamwork experience, and diverse understandings of project requirements. Teammates influence content development, and they are the first readers of each other's work. Empathizing with teammates is therefore as valuable as empathizing with audiences for whom they develop content.

Empathy is not only a starting place but a resource that needs renewal throughout the writing process. Teammates develop empathy through the Interest/Confidence Inventory, while developing a team charter, when writing team update memos, and during team retrospective meetings.

CHAPTER 5

⑦ Defining

Including time for problem definition helps teams come to a mutual understanding of project goals and obstacles. Defining problems accurately also helps teams avoid hasty decision making. Problem definition helps answer the question, "Interdependence how? Interdependence to what end?"

Defining problems and goals based on ideas from all teammates, and subjecting all ideas to discussion and assessment by comparing them to project objectives, is a valuable stage in the collaborative writing process.

Problem definition occurs during prewriting, while developing research questions, hypotheses, user stories, during increment reviews—sometimes resulting in problem re-definition, while drafting team updates memos, and during team retrospectives and peer review.

Successful collaborations often boil down to how well a team can articulate the problem at hand. We encourage teams to methodically define the problem that their projects charge them with addressing and the team problems that emerge while working on projects.

Problem definition occurs primarily during team update and team retrospective meetings.

CHAPTER 5

 Prototyping

An important step in further defining problems includes making visible each individual's understanding of the problem. Individual expressions may be verbal or visual, but all teammates should contribute if teams are to maximize the benefits of collaboration. Discussions about ideas in specific terms of course requirements for critical thinking, research, genre/structure, synthesis, and review/editing help teams discern the viability of ideas and directions for modifying them. Making ideas visible helps teams see connections among ideas and course requirements.

Making ideas visible occurs during prototyping, increment review, and memoing.

 Increment review

We have found an emphasis on targeted feedback (Ambrose et al., 2010) to be especially helpful in achieving goals for interdependent writing. In *How Learning Works*, the authors argue that "when practice and feedback are focused on the same aspects of students' performance, students have the chance to practice and refine a consistent body of new knowledge and skill" (p. 126). We have pursued that focus by aligning writing requirements with course-specific learning objectives and reiterating the requirements during generative activities, research and annotation activities, peer review, and evaluation activities. Figure 13 illustrates how targeted feedback based on reiterated requirements can take place throughout the collaborative writing process.

CHAPTER 5

Generative activities	Incremental review activities	Research / annotation activities	Co-authoring activities	Peer review activities
Critical Thinking	Critical Thinking	Critical Thinking	Critical Thinking	Critical Thinking
Research	Research	Research	Research	Research
Genre/Structure	Genre/Structure	Genre/Structure	Genre/Structure	Genre/Structure
Synthesis	Synthesis	Synthesis	Synthesis	Synthesis
Review/Editing	Review/Editing	Review/Editing	Review/Editing	Review/Editing

Figure 13. **Reiterating consistent learning objectives during collaborative writing projects promotes deep learning.**

CHAPTER 5

Subjecting ideas to review by classmates, teammates, instructor and, when possible, nonacademic audiences helps teams validate or redirect their efforts. Frequent review enables teammates to adapt to what they learn from others while they are engaged in content development rather than solely at the end of content development.

Instructor feedback to teams or the whole class during increment review is more efficient than feedback to individual students because instructors can address comments to everyone at the same time. During increment review, teammates reveal their understanding of key project requirements and in their responses instructors can reiterate key values and direction for revision. Discussing increments has the additional advantage of providing feedback prior to prolonged investment in gives teammates opportunities to meet frequently to build trust, share ideas, and test assumptions. Reviewing occurs during increment review and peer review.

Comparison: increments and drafts

Peer review of increments differs in several important ways from peer review of drafts. Both are valuable and each serves distinct purposes. Increment review should be brief and informal. Because increments may be a title, a heading, a few sentences, an image or any other content sample the team considers finished, they do not require prolonged investment from students to prepare or discuss when compared with drafts (Table 5.1). Increment review is, therefore, a low-stakes activity. However, because increment review takes place throughout the content-development process, it has the potential to have a powerful impact on team outcomes.

CHAPTER 5

Table 5.1. **Key differences between increments and drafts.**

	Increments	Drafts
Amount of content	Small	Large
Student and instructor investment (in time)	Low	High
Review frequency	Frequent	Infrequent
Duration of review	Short	Long

Increment review provides useful formative feedback while peer reviews are summative in nature. Because increment review occurs briefly but frequently, students, teammates, and instructor can efficiently exchange information about progress and productivity generally, and interpretation of requirements specifically. Over time, students and instructor "practice and refine a consistent body of new knowledge and skill" (Ambrose et al., 2010, p. 126).

Given the distinctive purposes of increment review and draft review, the structure of review activities also differs in several ways. Table 5.2 outlines the key differences and illustrates how both methods support student learning.

Table 5.2. **Formative increment review complements summative peer review in interdependent writing teams.**

	Team review of increments	Peer review of drafts
Who prepares	Teammates prepare and present increment reviews.	Readers prepare peer reviews after authors have finished developing content.
Who compares content to requirements	Teammates describe to an audience of teammates or classmates how they see increments representing achievement in project requirements.	Readers reflect back to authors how they see drafts representing achievement in project requirements.
Review visibility	Readers/listeners reflect back to teammates/classmates; their thinking is visible to instructor, team, or class.	Reader(s) reflect back to author(s). Their feedback is visible to authors.

Increment review activity

Purpose
The purpose of increment review is for teams to present representative content to the class and receive feedback.

Listening to what other teams are doing—and listening to the feedback other teams receive—gives you insight into requirements and which strategies for meeting them are working, in need of rethinking, or suggest new directions as you continue working together.

What is an increment?
An increment is a small part of your project. It can be a title, a purpose statement, an image with a caption, a paragraph—any small part that you consider finished. Select an increment that represents a contribution you've made to the project.

How should I discuss the increment?
Explain how the increment meets two of the numbered items for each of the five requirements listed below.

Critical thinking requirement

How does the increment
1. address an audience need?
2. support the purpose of the larger content of which it's a part?
3. contribute to the tone of the content?
4. contribute to reader trust in the content?
5. help define an important concept?

Research requirement

How does the increment meet requirements for
1. accurate, credible citations?
2. emphasizing human impact?
3. presenting information in cause/effect form?
4. making claims?
5. supporting claims with valid information?

Genre/structure requirement

How does the increment
    1. represent content that addresses readers' needs and interests?
    2. address readers' values?
    3. represent formatting that aids users in finding information they need quickly?
    4. represent visual elements that meet readers' needs and interests?
    5. represent the requirement for descriptive captions for all figures and tables?

Synthesis requirement

How does the increment
    1. accurately paraphrase source information?
    2. represent collaborative thinking?
    3. includes signal phrases describing the credibility of sources?
    4. evaluate information to aid readers' understanding?
    5. represent an original conclusion you've drawn from source material?

Review and editing requirement

How does the increment
    1. present consistent word choice?
    2. support your goal of presenting information in a professional way?
    3. support the goal of avoiding distracting patterns of error?
    4. demonstrate adherence to professional publishing standards for clarity, accuracy, or consistency?
    5. represent collaborative editing, review, or revision?

Teamwork requirement

How does the increment represent team achievement in
    1. participation?
    2. cooperation?
    3. collaboration?
    4. working together outside of class?
    5. overcoming obstacles?

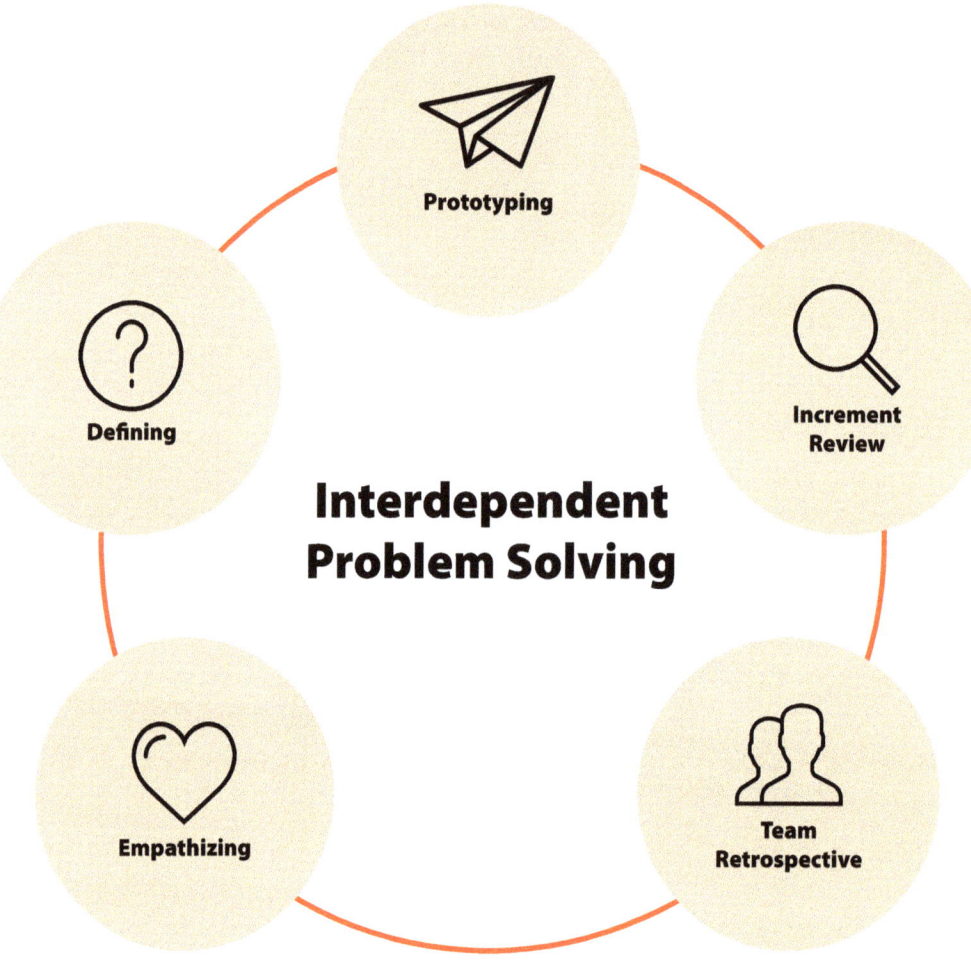

Figure 14. **Components of an interdependent problem-solving framework.**

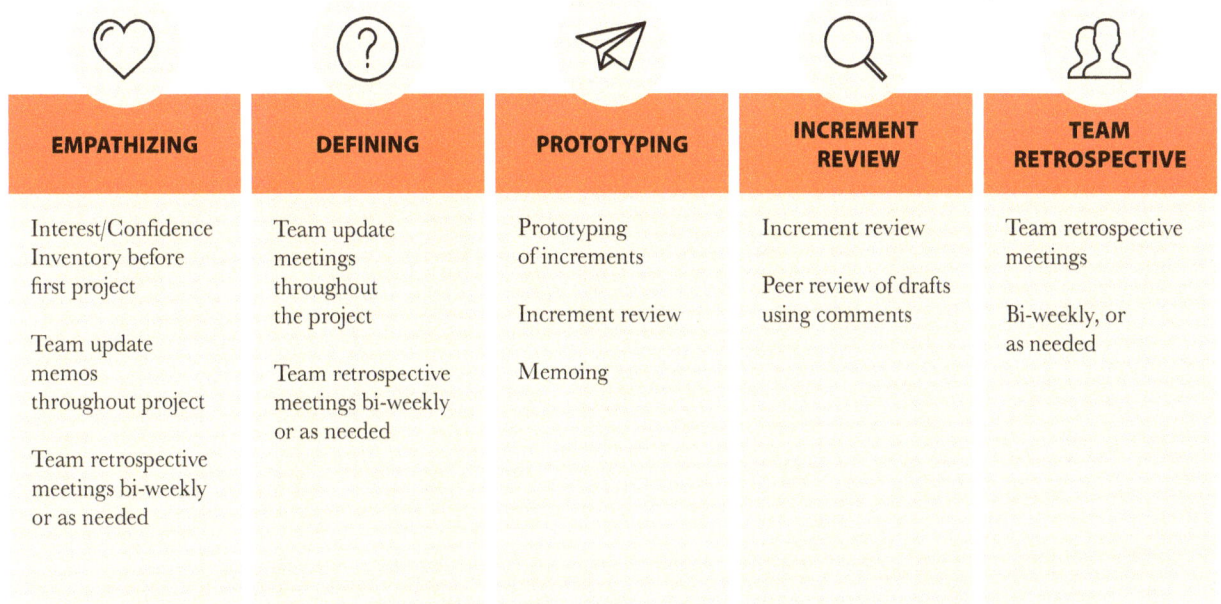

Figure 15. **Associated activities in interdependent problem solving.**

CHAPTER 5

The following outline for interdependent peer review provides response guidelines for students. The guidelines align with writing requirements that support course learning objectives in collaborative writing projects.

> In your role for peer review, discuss how the content you're reviewing can more thoroughly address requirements.
>
> **Critical thinking requirements**
>
> - Uses an appropriate tone: factual, professional (not colloquial).
> - Content includes a statement about its purpose or focus.
> - Content maintains reader trust by citing valid sources as required.
> - The work defines terms as required.
> - The work includes a statement about key audience(s) and content is appropriate to its audience(s).
>
> **Research requirements**
>
> - Includes signal phrases, paraphrases, and in-text citations as required.
> - Includes a list of references as required.
> - Explains or illustrates human impact as required.
> - The work discusses cause and effect as required.
> - The work includes claims and valid support.
> - References are in alphabetical order by first word of the citation.
>
> **Genre/structure requirements**
>
> - The work meets requirements for length, depth, and breadth.
> - The work includes visuals as required.
>   » Includes table and image numbers, captions, and citations as required.
> - Includes introductory information as required.
> - Includes definitions of terms as required.
> - Headings and captions are descriptive of the content they refer to (no one-word headings).
> - Includes all content sections.
> - Meets content organization requirements.

CHAPTER 5

Synthesis requirements

- Includes topic sentence claims.
- Includes signal phrases, paraphrases, and citations as required.
    » Signal phrases indicate source validity.
    » Paraphrases interpret information from the source material.
    » Paraphrases support topic sentence claims.
    » Paraphrases end with source citations as assigned.
- Paragraphs include comments about the value or significance of paragraph content as it relates to a thesis or other key idea.

Review/editing requirements

- Wording is consistent throughout.
- Content is free of distracting errors.
- Each teammate has made the required number of comments or suggestions.
- Content sections included; paragraphs fully developed.
- Source information is cited, reference lists meet requirements.

Redundancy on purpose

Building some redundancy into peer review tasks supports interdependent peer review. For example, duplicating peer review tasks for the research and genre/structure roles supports interdependence by requiring teammates to perform the same tasks from two teammates' perspectives. When teammates review with the same purpose in mind, they are likely to respond differently to different content. Differences in response and opinion among teammates should lead to conversations about the significance and purpose of writing requirements.

CHAPTER 5

 Team retrospective

Teams do not recognize or realize interdependence right away. Exploring team processes and reflecting on their effectiveness gives teams a chance to continuously improve their work together. Periodic discussions about what's working, what's not working—often in terms of teammate communication, cooperation, and timeliness but also in terms of teammate understanding of priorities and requirements—help teams determine what they should continue doing, stop doing, and modify in order to align future efforts with project-specific goals.

Retrospectives occur periodically—bi-weekly, or as needed— to help teams identify what's working, what's not working, and how they can proceed together more productively right away.

CHAPTER 6

CREATE A VISION FOR COLLABORATIVE WRITING

GUIDING QUESTIONS

- How should I design projects for interdependent collaborative writing teams?
- What are the parts of a project vision?

CHAPTER 6

A project vision is the guide you create to give students and teams the direction they need while pursuing course learning objectives together.

Hope for the best, plan for the best

The instructor contributes to the success of team projects by balancing project requirements with learning activities that support team productivity. Therefore, the project vision describes the purpose of the project, which materials teams should create together, the learning objectives of the project, and how project elements contribute to student learning. It describes in some detail how teams should work together to achieve their goals and how project elements support their goals.

Having a detailed vision promotes teammate interdependence by illustrating the complexity of the project at the outset while providing support for managing complexity in teams. The vision also supports the instructor in making choices about what to require of students and how best to support student success.

Summarize audience, content, and purpose of the project

Whether you begin or end the vision-making process with a summary, creating one is a helpful process of reflection about key project goals. For students, a project summary is a valuable touchstone when project details compete for attention. Table 6.1 shows an example project summary for a feasibility report.

Table 6.1. **Collaborative writing project vision for a feasibility report. Goal is to give readers a basis for decision making.**

Audience(s)	Audience needs	Content (final product)	Purpose of final product
Decision makers who must determine the feasibility of a particular course of action for achieving a particular goal.	Research-based information about the feasibility of a specific course of action.	15-page report formatted as a feasibility report, with headings Introduction, Methods, Results, Discussion.	Give readers a factual basis for moving forward or not moving forward on a particular course of action.

CHAPTER 6

The remainder of this chapter outlines content for a complete project vision. *[Items in brackets indicate examples.]*

Project number or title: [   ]

A. Summary

Include the project duration, number and genre of works, the learning each work should demonstrate, and the audience for works. Example:

> In this *[4-week]* project, each team will co-author *[1 proposal, 1 feasibility report, and 1 memo of transmittal]* to demonstrate learning and skills in *[research, analysis, and working cooperatively in teams]*. Your audience is *[your instructor and a decision-maker that you designate]*.

Sketch your project summary here.

CHAPTER 6

B. Audience needs and goals

Help students imagine real readers who need project materials to meet their goals.

Example 1: *[Hiring managers]* who *[want to see evidence of]* your achievement as *[a communicator and as a team player]*.

> "As a hiring manager, I want to see evidence of your success as a problem solver so I can determine how much training you will need."

Example 2: Your instructor, who wants *[to evaluate your work according to course goals]*.

> "As an instructor, I want to see evidence of your knowledge of course content and disciplinary writing so I can assess your progress."

Example 3: A decision-maker who needs the information in order to *[decide on the feasibility of a specific course of action]*.

> "As a community organizer, I need current research on youth programming that specifically encourages activism for high-school completion and college entry. What is a feasible program design for our community?"

Sketch a sample statement of audience needs and goals here.

CHAPTER 6

C. Project value

Describe the value of the project in terms of student learning. Example:

> Students who complete this project will deepen their knowledge of *[topic, research, analysis, and synthesis]*.

Sketch a few project values here.

CHAPTER 6

D. Distinguishing features of the project and final product(s)

Help students understand the project by comparing and contrasting it with others with which they may already be familiar. Examples:

> Perhaps unlike projects for other courses, this project asks you to _____. Also perhaps different from other projects, _____.
>
> This project requires collaborative writing in which teams work together to meet these specific goals:
>
> 1. *[Peer review each other's work with specific project objectives in mind.]*
> 2. *[Make significant contributions to process, drafts, final products, and team productivity.]*

Sketch some distinguishable features of your project here.

CHAPTER 6

E. Purpose of the final product(s)

Explain the purpose of the final written products to help students imagine real readers for their work.

> Example 1: A reader of *[work name or genre]* will read your work in order to make decisions about _____.

> Example 2: When finished, the work you produce for this project could be shared with a potential employer to demonstrate your professional development in _____, including teamwork and project coordination.

> Example 3: When finished, your work should demonstrate knowledge of _____.

> Example 4: Content for this project must _____.

Sketch a purpose of the final product here.

CHAPTER 6

F. Project learning objectives

What do you want students to learn? What should they be able to do as a result of completing the project? Include key objectives such as critical thinking, research, genre/structure, synthesis, review/editing, or other key learning objectives for the project.

Explain the critical thinking objectives of the project. Start with a definition of critical thinking that aligns with your course goals. Example:

> To demonstrate achievement in critical thinking, your *[writing, your annotations, and your reflections about assigned readings]* should include observations about *[audience, tone, purpose, main argument, counter-argument, interpretation, and evaluation]*.

Explain the research objectives of the project. Example:

> To demonstrate achievement in research, *[you should craft a focused research question, a preliminary hypothesis, a plan for using valid sources, and use of an approved citation style]*.

CHAPTER 6

Explain the genre and structure objectives for the work(s). Example:

> Project 2 must consist of *[all digital materials...]*.

Discuss specific genre/structure/section objectives. Examples:

- Front matter objectives: table of contents, title page, abstract
- Introduction objectives
- Main headings or sections
- IMRaD structure
- Specific genre objectives
- Captioning objectives
- Back matter: content you require that doesn't belong in the main content

Explain the synthesis objectives of the project:

> What does effective synthesis look like in your course? One model of synthesis asks students to make claims, support claims with valid sources (accurately paraphrased or appropriately quoted), using a course specific citation style, and drawing original conclusions from source material.

Explain the review/editing objectives of the project. Examples:

> Outline your guidelines for peer review. For instance, how often will teammates and instructor review content and provide feedback?

> What will teammates and instructor review: several increments (recommended), one draft, two drafts, or other?

Sketch your project learning objectives here.

CHAPTER 6

G. Resources

List resources that support course and writing goals. Examples: writing templates, assigned readings, and models of items submitted from past courses.

> Sketch some resources you might provide to students here.

H. How to decide on a topic and divide the work

Will you assign a topic or ask teams to arrive at a topic that interests them? Explain here.

> What are the pros and cons of assigning topics?

CHAPTER 6

I. Who is responsible for a student's grade?

Explain how you will grade individuals and teams and how or whether an individual's performance affects teammate grades.

Options include:
- Individual grades for specific written contributions.
- Individual grades for contributions to team discussions.
- Individual grades for contributions to project documentation.
- Team grades for efforts that result in, for example:
    » Compliance with teammates' requests (high achievement in cooperation).
    » Working toward shared goals (high achievement in collaboration).

Sketch other ideas for grading individuals and teams here.

CHAPTER 6

J. How do teammates influence student grade?

Explain the influence that teammates have on individual grades. Example:

> Teams influence your grade by providing multiple perspectives on your work and providing feedback from those multiple points of view. For example, using the five categories of objectives, teammate who provide feedback influence your grades in the following ways:
>
> - by offering reminders about specific objectives (increasing your productivity);
> - by interpreting objectives differently from you (increasing understanding of objectives and how to meet them);
> - by making specific suggestions for improvement (increasing the value of your writing); and
> - by letting you know how others perceive your writing (increasing your empathy).

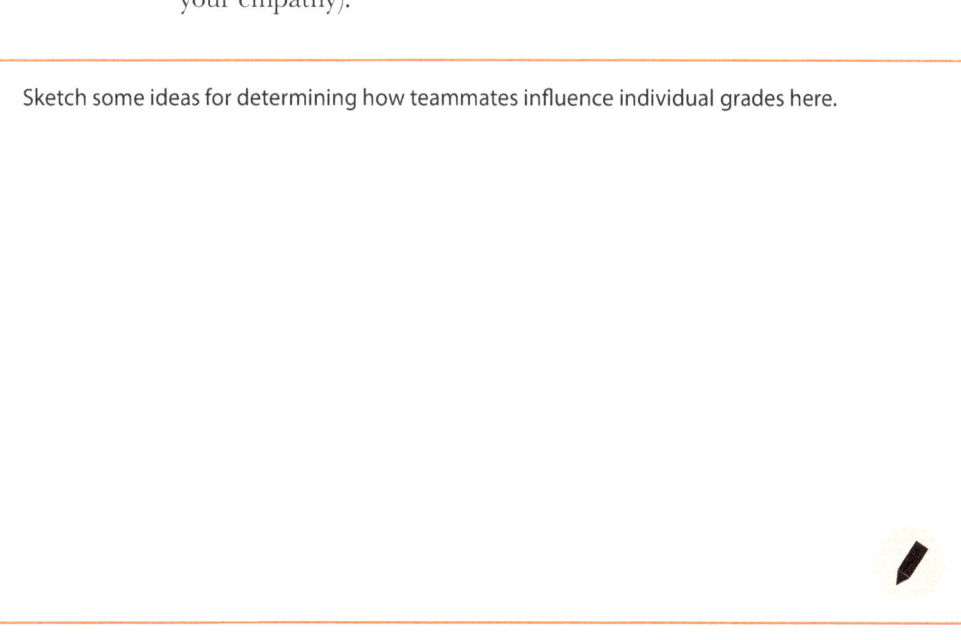

Sketch some ideas for determining how teammates influence individual grades here.

CHAPTER 6

K. How will you evaluate individual work?

Explain the weight of the project (percentage of course grade) and how you will evaluate the team and the content. Align grading with course learning objectives to convey the value of writing within the course and the discipline.

Here is a sample basic objectives and grade breakdown.

Table 6.2. **Sample breakdown of project grade percentage for each objective.**

Project Objectives	% of project grade	Definition
Critical thinking	16%	Meet objectives for [audience, purpose, tone, trust, interpretation, and evaluation].
Research	16%	Include [research question, hypothesis, valid sources].
Genre/structure	16%	Meet genre/structure objectives for the project, [including content headings and all assigned content sections].
Synthesis	16%	Meet objectives for [making original contributions to projects, drawing original conclusions from source content.]
Review & editing	16%	Provide detailed and useful feedback, make substantive and valuable revisions, and proofread.
Team participation	20%	Make identifiable, valuable contributions to your team's work during all phases of the project.

CHAPTER 6

L. Project calendar

Indicate key writing deadlines and activities. Team-based writing projects typically include scheduling for brief team updates about the assignment, feedback reviews, and team retrospectives about communication and productivity.

Here is a refresher from Chapter 5:

Table 6.3. **Sample activities in our problem-solving framework.**

Problem-solving framework	Sample activities
Empathizing	Interest/Confidence Inventory before first project Team charter before first project Team update memos throughout project Team retrospective meetings bi-weekly or as needed
Defining	Team update meetings throughout the project Team retrospective meetings bi-weekly or as needed
Prototyping	Prototyping of increments Increment review Memoing
Increment review	Increment review Peer review of drafts using objective-specific comments
Team retrospective	Team retrospective meetings Bi-weekly, or as needed

CHAPTER 6

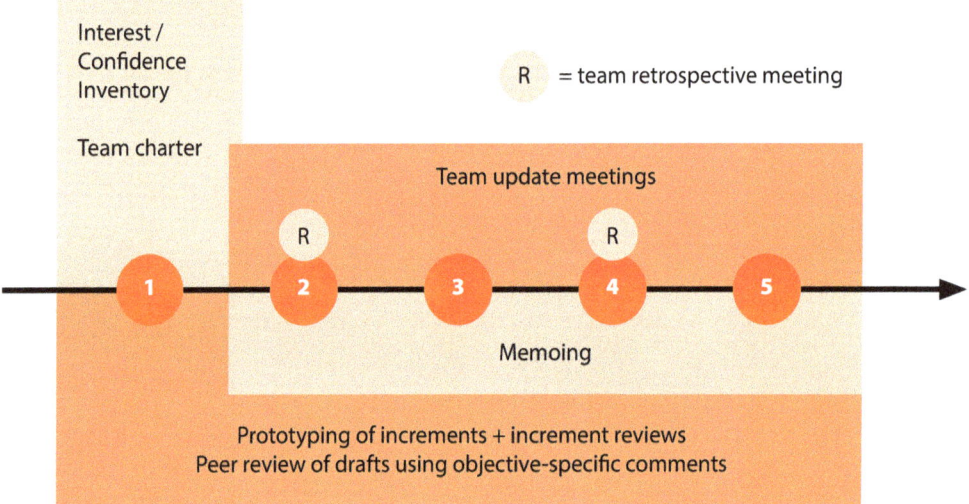

Figure 16. **5-week project sample schedule.**

CHAPTER 6

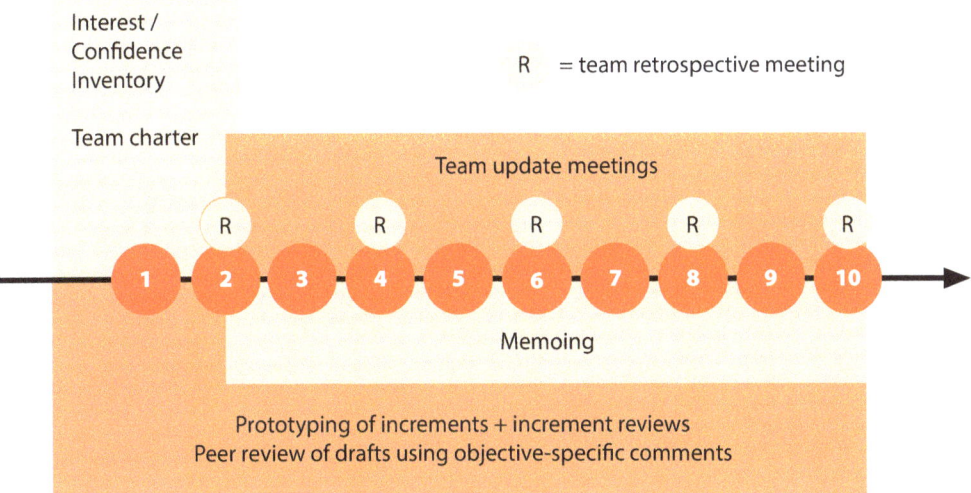

Figure 17. **10-week project sample schedule.**

CHAPTER 6

Design your semester-long project schedule.

CHAPTER 6

COLLABORATIVE WRITING PLAYBOOK

Final words

We end our current discussion about collaborative writing with a student's observation that inspires our ongoing interest in collaborative writing as a mode of learning:

> *"Interacting and working with my team has been a highlight of my years here. I've been able to combine learning with teamwork and healthy stress management in a way that has been understanding, flexible, and highly rewarding."*

As a team of two, we share the student's view that thinking and writing together has been a highlight of our professional lives, standing out for the many rewards of having ideas first trusted and valued and then subject to our own evolving understanding of what collaborative writing is and can be.

Figure 18. **The Playbook authors: Jason Tham (left) and Joe Moses (right).**

REFERENCES

African American & African Studies. (2010). University of Minnesota Writing Plan. Retrieved from https://bit.ly/3u0dVcN

Ambrose, S. A., et al. (2010). *How learning works: Seven research-based principles for smart teaching.* New York, NY: John Wiley & Sons. Retrieved from ProQuest Ebook Central, https://bit.ly/2ZkTqZV.

Brewer, J.D., & Klein, S., (2006). Type of positive interdependence and affiliation motive in an asynchronous, collaborative learning environment. *Educational Technology Research and Development 54*(4), 331–354.

Brumberger, E., & Lauer, C. (2015). The evolution of technical communication: An analysis of industry job postings. *Technical Communication, 62*(4), 224–243.

Burnett, R.E., White, C.I., and Duin, A.H. (1997). Locating collaboration: Reflections, features, and influences. In C.M. Ornatowski and K. Staples (Eds.), *Theory, practice, and program design in technical communication: Foundations for teaching an emergent discipline* (pp. 133–160). Norwood, NJ: Ablex Publishers.

Carr, P.B. & Walton, G.M. (2014). Cues of working together fuel intrinsic motivation. *Journal of Experimental Social Psychology, 53*, 169–184.

College of Biological Sciences. (2017). University of Minnesota Writing Plan. Retrieved from https://bit.ly/3rXE1v0.

Communication Studies. (2019). Learning objectives. University of Minnesota. Retrieved from http://bit.ly/3u2ED4l.

Deloitte. (2016). *The new organization: Different by design.* Deloitte global human capital trends. Deloitte Insights. Retrieved from http://bit.ly/3do2yoX.

Deloitte. (2018). *The rise of the social enterprise.* Deloitte global human capital trends. Deloitte Insights. Retrieved from https://bit.ly/3avlgcF.

Dicks, S. (2013). How can technical communicators manage projects? In J. Johnson-Eilola & S. Selber (Eds.), *Solving problems in technical communication* (pp. 310–335). Chicago, IL: The University of Chicago Press.

Ede L. & Lunsford A. (1990). *Singular texts/plural authors: Perspectives on collaborative authoring.* Carbondale, IL: Southern Illinois University Press.

Johnson, D. W., Johnson, R. T., & Smith, K. A. (1991). *Cooperative learning: Increasing college faculty instructional productivity* (ASHE-ERIC Higher Education Report No. 4). Washington, DC: The George Washington University, School of Education and Human Development.

Johnson, D. W., Johnson, R. T., & Smith, K. A. (2007). The state of cooperative learning In postsecondary and professional settings. *Educational Psychology Review, 19*, 15–29.

Johnson, D. W., Johnson, R. T., Smith, K. A. (2014). Cooperative learning: Improving university instruction by basing practice on validated theory. *Journal on Excellence in College Teaching, 25*(3&4), 85–118.

Keyes, R. (1995). *The courage to write: How writers transcend fear.* New York, NY: Henry Holt.

Lowry, P.B., Curtis, A., & Lowry, M.R. (2004). Building a taxonomy and nomenclature of collaborative writing to improve interdisciplinary research and practice. *International Journal of Business Communication, 41*(1), 66–99.

Marback, R. (2009). Embracing wicked problems: the turn to design in composition studies. *College Composition and Communication, 61*(2), W397–W419.

Nordmark, M. (2017). Writing roles: A model for understanding students' digital writing and the positions that they adopt as writers. *Computers and Composition, 46*, 56–71.

Page, D., & Donelan, J.G., (2003). Team-building tools for students. *Journal of Education for Business, 78*(3), 125–128.

Pope-Ruark, R. (2012). We scrum every day: using scrum project management framework for group projects. *College Teaching, 60*(4), 164–169.

Pope-Ruark, R. (2015). Introducing agile project management strategies in technical and professional communication courses. *Journal of Business and Technical Communication, 29*(1), 112–133.

Pope-Ruark, R., Tham, J., Moses, J., Conner, T. (Eds.). (2019). Design-thinking approaches in technical and professional communication. [Special issue]. *Journal of Business and Technical Communication, 33*(4), 370–465.

Purdy, J.P. (2014). What can design thinking offer writing studies? *College Composition and Communication, 65*(4), 612–641.

Smith, P. & Krumsieg, K. (2003). Designing teams and assigning roles. *Faculty Development Series*, 147–150. Retrieved from https://bit.ly/37kQ5OV.

Theater Arts and Dance. (2015). University of Minnesota Writing Plan. Retrieved from https://bit.ly/3pkGj5K.

Writing Enriched Curriculum Program. (2011–2019). University of Minnesota. Writing Plans. Retrieved from http://bit.ly/3dgjwWp.

KEYWORDS

Adaptation
A core principle of collaborative writing, adaptation means being open to change so teams can apply learning and revise their work processes based on emergent team and audience needs.

Collaborative writing project
Structured activities for teammates in writing roles that complement course-specific learning objectives.

Design thinking
A framework for problem definition in collaborative writing.

Empathy
Understanding writing, problems, topics, objectives, and course content from someone else's point of view, including teammates'.

Ideation
Generating and visualizing ideas from all teammates.

Increments
Short passages (titles, headings, paragraphs, sentences) that individuals or teams consider finished and ready for review.

Objectives
Any learning outcome you expect students to demonstrate in their writing; may include goals for learning about course content or about writing.

Problem definition
The result of collaboratively considering problems from multiple perspectives.

Prototyping
Making quick, rough visualizations of a tentative solution for discussion and review.

KEYWORDS

Review
A core principle of collaborative writing, review means sustaining an environment of continuous improvement through review of written increments and evaluation of team productivity.

Retrospective meetings
Team meetings in which teammates discuss what's working well in terms of productivity, what isn't working well, and change they will make to improve productivity.

Tasks
Activities students conduct in order to meet project objectives.

Team update meetings
Brief informal team meetings in which teammates discuss what they've worked on since their last team update meeting, what they plan to finish by the next meeting, and what obstacles they have encountered since the last meeting and are likely to encounter before the next. May result in a team update memo.

Transparency
A core principle of collaborative writing, transparency means creating an environment in which students and instructor "make thinking visible" by sharing and discussing their writing objectives, ideas about projects, and project expectations.

Vision
A foundational document containing project objectives, purpose, and timeline.

www.ingramcontent.com/pod-product-compliance
Lightning Source LLC
Chambersburg PA
CBHW040931240426
43672CB00022B/2999